At the Water's Edge
WADING BIRDS OF NORTH AMERICA

John Netherton
Foreword by John C. Ogden

Voyageur Press

Printed in Hong Kong
94 95 96 97 98   5 4 3 2 1

Please write or call, or stop by, for our free catalog of natural history publications. Our toll-free number to place an order or to obtain a free catalog is 800-888-9653.

Educators, fundraisers, premium and gift buyers, publicists, and marketing managers: Looking for creative products and new sales ideas? Voyageur Press books are available at special discounts when purchased in quantities, and special editions can be created to your specifications. For details contact the marketing department.

Library of Congress Cataloging-in-Publication Data
Netherton, John.
   At the water's edge : wading birds of North America / by John Netherton.
     p. cm.
   Includes bibliographical references and index.
   ISBN 0-89658-233-7
   1. Ciconiiformes—North America. 2. Gruiformes—North America. 3. Wildlife viewing sites—United States. I. Title.
   QL696.C5N47   1994
   598.3'4097—dc20   93–21365
                    CIP

Published by **VOYAGEUR PRESS, INC.**
P.O. Box 338, 123 North Second Street
Stillwater, MN 55082 U.S.A. ∾ 612-430-2210

Distributed in Canada through **RAINCOAST BOOKS**
112 East Third Avenue
Vancouver, B.C. V5T 1C8

PICTURED ON THE FRONT COVER: *tricolored heron.* BACK COVER: *roseate spoonbill wading in early morning; great egret; little blue heron watching fish swim within striking range; green-backed heron uttering its familiar* skeow *cry before taking flight.* PAGE 1: *A great egret stands motionless, peering into the calm waters of a small pond.* PAGES 2–3: *Great blue herons find the shores of shallow lakes excellent feeding areas. These large birds prefer to stand motionless for long periods waiting for potential prey to approach them.* PAGE 4 (ABOVE): *Nesting areas can create tight quarters for different species, triggering conflicts.*

PAGE 5 (OPPOSITE): *When snowies are quite young, their parents regurgitate predigested food directly into the nest, then pick up chunks and place them into the young birds' mouths.* PAGE 6: *A cattle egret sits on her nest a few feet above water. When taking up residence in mixed colonies, these little birds often are forced to nest lower in the branches or further inside the tangled growth.* PAGE 7 (CONTENTS): *The great blue flies in typical heron fashion with its head tucked back on its shoulders and its long legs trailing behind. The great blue frequently robs smaller herons and egrets of their freshly caught food.*

Dedication

For my loving wife, Judy, and my wonderful children, Jason, Joshua, Erich, Joshua, and Evan

Acknowledgments

I would like to thank everyone who helped to bring this book to fruition: David Badger, Herbert Bell, Doug Benson, Bruce Blihovde, Forrest Cameron, Frank Carroll, Donald Clapp, Jim Clark, Charles Coppedge, Mike Farmer, Brent Giezentanner, Jerry Gingerich, Walker Golder, Albert Hight, Louis Hinds, Charlie Jarman, Mark Kays, Mike Kirk, Greg Lepera, Wayne Lindsey, LeMoyne Marlatt, Nancy Marx, Will Nidecker, Nikon Inc., Philip Norton, John Ogden, David Olsen, Rich Paul, Steve Reef, Ben Roche, Gary Stolz, John Turner, and Jim Wells.

Contents

Foreword

My earliest notion about long-legged wading birds was that they were to be encountered only in the hot, steamy swamps of the southern states. So on my first Christmas Bird Count, when I was assigned the task of locating a previously reported day roost of black-crowned night-herons in woods along the banks of the Cumberland River, Tennessee, I wasn't convinced that the count leader knew what he was talking about. The day was subfreezing, with gusty winds and light sleet. After an hour of searching without success, I was even more certain that not only were there no herons in such an environment, but that the day was cold enough that I had no business being there either. Moments later, the huddled, gray forms of twenty night-herons were spotted, clustered on low perches in the bare branches of a hackberry thicket. As I later learned, in spite of my notions, night-herons had been wintering along this stretch of the river for as long as people could remember.

Some years later, in part to avoid being in cold places, I got a job as a wildlife biologist at Everglades National Park in Florida. There I studied wood storks in an environment that I considered to be a more typical habitat for wading birds, one that was about equal parts humidity, mud, mangrove roots, and mosquitoes. Add the pungent odor of regurgitated fish and layers of "whitewash" around the nests in the colonies, and the image becomes even sharper. It was here that I had it reaffirmed that these hot places are of special importance, if not for all wading birds, then certainly for large numbers of them. In fact, it was the tremendous numbers of snowy and great egrets, tricolored and great blue herons, and white ibis and wood storks fifty years ago that played a major role in the creation of the national park.

The truth is that wading birds occur in many different places and habitats, and that each species has some require-ments that are different from the others. We have studied storks and other wading birds in the Everglades because knowledge about the specific habitat requirements of each species provides us with one means of evaluating how water-management practices outside the park have impacted animals and ecosystems within our boundaries. Wading birds are quick to respond to changes in such environmental variables as food abundance, water depth, flooding and drying rates, and the seasonal timing of hydrological events. Typically the birds respond by changing what they do: when and where they nest, how many pairs nest in each colony, how many young are raised, and even by changing the number of birds feeding in a region, sometimes very abruptly. And because most wading birds are large and showy, they are easy to locate and count. If a nesting colony remains in the same place for many years, as is true for several that are described in this book, then it can be assumed that habitat conditions around that colony are good for the birds. But as has happened in too many places, including Everglades National Park, recent years have seen the disappearance of one colony after another. These losses usually mean that the wetlands that are essential feeding habitats for wading birds and other animals have been drained or polluted. The birds move elsewhere, or they die and are not replaced.

It is so important for us to recognize the beauty of wading birds and other creatures that depend on our disappearing wetlands, and to know something about these birds and what their actions tell us about our own world. John Netherton's photographs and text are just the ticket for full admission into the life of wading birds, for both the first-time and repeat visitor. Once you have explored these pages, I hope that you will have a new appreciation for those Southern swamps—and for protecting that small, local marsh or pond.

John C. Ogden, Wildlife Biologist
Homestead, Florida

A sandhill crane is silhouetted in a marsh in New Mexico. As the sun rises, the bird will fly off for the day to feed, then return in the evening just at sunset.

Introduction

My first encounter with wading birds came early one February morning on the edge of Mrazek Pond in Florida's Everglades National Park. The pond was shrouded in fog when, suddenly, hundreds of egrets, herons, and spoonbills flew in and landed on the shallow water teeming with minnows and tiny crustaceans. Tricolored herons dashed about, their wings spread to form canopies. Slender snowy egrets stirred the muddy bottom in search of prey and from time to time flew low over the water's surface, dipping their bright yellow feet into the pond to grab small fish startled by the birds' acrobatics. Great egrets stood motionless for minutes at a time, then thrust their sharp bills into the water with lightning speed, impaling their prey. Magnificent roseate spoonbills walked within a foot or two of where I sat, swinging their spatulate bills from side to side in a graceful arclike motion. One spoonbill even flew so low over my head that it grazed my hair with its primary feathers before landing just behind me.

Experiences such as these are truly rare. The setting itself was primal; the sensations were exhilarating. This event, in fact, would be the catalyst for my returning to the Everglades every winter for the next twenty-five years. On each trip I would learn a little more about the unique characteristics of each species of wading bird, large birds that have adapted to wading in shallow water by evolving long legs, necks, and bills. While at the Everglades, I noted catastrophic effects caused by humans or nature on the birds' populations over time.

I have seen the Everglades through some of its worst recorded droughts. I have watched as the area was flooded when canals were opened to rid agricultural and residential areas of too much rain. I have observed the wildlife through the ban on DDT. I have seen marshes drained to create residential areas and shopping malls. In 1936, there were 6.97 million acres of marshland in Florida. By 1987, there were only 3.09 million acres. In 1870, the estimated population of wading birds in South Florida was 2.5 million. That population plunged to 500,000 after the arrival of the plume hunters in the mid-nineteenth century. These hunters primarily sought the prized white nuptial feathers of the great and snowy egrets, which, according to Everglades historian Marjory Stoneman Douglas, brought 75 cents apiece in New York after the Civil War. In 1877, the Florida legislature prohibited the killing of these birds, but the laws were widely circumvented. Finally, in 1900, the Lacey Act outlawed interstate transportation of illegally killed birds, and the Migratory Bird Act of 1913 forbade commercial sales of most native birds. After plume hunting was outlawed, the numbers increased to 1.2 million by 1935. Unfortunately, our unceasing drainage of the wetlands reduced the numbers to a mere 130,000 birds by 1975. In their impact study, James Kushlan and D. A. White confirmed not only an urgent need for protection of Florida's wetlands but also the negative global effects of losing vital marshes.

President Theodore Roosevelt demonstrated enormous foresight in 1903, when he created Pelican Island, Florida, as the first national wildlife refuge. Today, there are over ninety million acres of land and water in the nearly 450 refuges throughout the United States. The National Audubon Society manages more than one hundred sanctuaries with more than 150,000 acres. Organizations such as The Land Trust Alliance and The Nature Conservancy look to the future to provide suitable habitats not only for wading birds, but for all species.

In this book, I have listed a number of locales, such as national wildlife refuges and National Audubon Society sanctuaries, which are of prime importance for the birds,

The term "wading bird" is often reserved for herons, egrets, ibises, spoonbills, and storks, but its general meaning includes large birds that have adapted to wading in shallow water by evolving long legs, necks, and bills. Waterfowl, such as ducks and geese, do not fall into this category. Pictured are tricolored herons.

and areas in which particular species can be viewed. I have written descriptions and natural histories of every major species of wading bird to acquaint the reader with the habits and eccentricities of these magnificent birds.

As humans continue to encroach on the wetlands, wading birds have had to adapt. No better example exists than the nesting rookery at the St. Augustine Alligator Farm in Florida, where the birds put up with thousands of tourists within a few feet of their nests just to secure a predator-free environment.

Unfortunately, not all wildlife can adapt so readily. We have entered a decade that is critical for the environment, in which decisions made will affect not only our generation, but also our children and their children. A Teton Sioux named Shooter once declared:

> All living creatures and all plants are a benefit to something. Certain animals fulfill their purpose by definite acts. The crows, buzzards and flies are somewhat similar in their use, and even the snakes have purpose in being. In the early days the animals probably roamed over a very wide country until they found a proper place.
>
> An animal depends a great deal on the natural conditions around it. If the buffalo were here today, I think they would be different from the buffalo of the old days because all the natural conditions have changed. They would not find the same food, nor the same surroundings. We see the changes in our ponies. In the old days they could stand great hardship and travel long distance without water. They lived on certain kinds of food and drank pure water. Now our horses require a mixture of food; they have less endurance and must have constant care.

We are now the stewards of our own planet. Every citizen can assume an active role and contribute to the preservation of the earth. And readers of this book can, I hope, experience the morning I was so fortunate to witness twenty-five years ago.

A great egret foraging for food in the Everglades' Mrazek Pond.

LEFT: *The roseate spoonbill has a sensitive spoon-shaped beak, which it inserts in the water and moves back and forth. When the beak touches a fish or other prey, it quickly snaps shut. The bird then tosses its victim into the air and swallows it whole. After feeding, spoonbills may stand and preen for twenty to thirty minutes before flying off to a roost.* INSET TOP: *An adult and young glossy ibis stand together in a drainage ditch where they feed. The young bird exhibits more greenish color with white down its neck, while the adult's coloring is more mahogany and green.* ABOVE: *A small great blue heron nesting area is silhouetted against the backdrop of Venice, Florida. Encroachment by humans on this wading bird's natural habitat is forcing the birds to adapt or perish.*

ABOVE: *Two Florida sandhill cranes wade through the sawgrass marshes of the Everglades. Florida sandhills are nonmigratory birds and tend to be seen in the same areas throughout the year.* LEFT: *Great blues are not typically seen in deep water, but the birds are excellent swimmers as long as they don't become waterlogged.*

Wading Bird Classification

Order: Ciconiiformes

    Family: Ardeidae

        Species: *Ardea herodias,* Great Blue Heron

            Ardea herodias occidentalis, Great White Heron

            Casmerodius albus, Great Egret

            Egretta thula, Snowy Egret

            Egretta caerulea, Little Blue Heron

            Egretta tricolor, Tricolored Heron

            Egretta rufescens, Reddish Egret

            Bubulcus ibis, Cattle Egret

            Nycticorax nycticorax, Black-crowned Night-Heron

            Butorides striatus, Green-backed Heron

            Nycticorax violaceus, Yellow-crowned Night-Heron (Note: The scientific name for this bird is expected to change to *Nyctanassa violaceus* in the upcoming edition of the American Ornithological Union's *Checklist.*)

    Family: Threskiornithidae

        Species: *Eudocimus albus,* White Ibis

            Plagadis falcinellus, Glossy Ibis

            Plegadis chihi, White-faced Ibis

            Ajaia ajaja, Roseate Spoonbill

    Family: Ciconiidae

        Species: *Mycteria americana,* Wood Stork

Order: Gruiformes

    Family: Aramidae

        Species: *Aramus guarauna,* Limpkin

    Family: Gruidae

        Species: *Grus canadensis,* Sandhill Crane

            Grus americana, Whooping Crane

A great blue heron stands atop its roost at sunset, defending its claimed area from hundreds of egrets and herons flying in for the night.

Great Blue Heron
ARDEA HERODIAS

Silhouetted in the early morning fog on a lake's edge or in vanishing wetlands, the stately great blue heron is a common sight. Largest of the North American herons, the great blue heron stands about four feet tall and weighs from six to eight pounds. The male is slightly larger than the female; otherwise, most birders find it virtually impossible to distinguish between sexes unless observing mating, when the female is on the bottom, or witnessing nest building, when the female receives the nesting twigs from the male as she constructs the nest. ● Great blue herons have long, thin necks and long blackish legs and feet. Their plumage is primarily gray, with a white crown and cheeks; a black stripe runs from near the bird's eye across the side of its crown. The underside of the great blue heron's neck is white, black, and brown, and the thigh feathers are rust-colored. Its bill is an orange-yellow, and its irises are yellow. ● During the great blue heron's courtship, the spaces between the beak and the eyes, called the "lores" (which are usually gray-green) change to blue. In addition, its dark legs change to a salmon color, and its black occipital plumes become more pronounced. In flight, the black primary and secondary feathers are prominently displayed. The great blue flies with its head pulled back on its shoulders, enabling onlookers to differentiate between the heron and the sandhill crane, which flies with its neck fully extended. Once in the air, the heron's wing beats are slow. When the bird lands, its seventy-inch wingspan becomes apparent, for it slows itself to a near stop with long legs outstretched as it locks its feet onto a branch. ● Except when roosting or nesting, great blues are fairly solitary. When ready to nest, the male will stand on an old nest, if one is available, and exhibit the customary stretch display—first pointing its bill skyward, then thrusting its head downward—to attract a mate. The nest may be solitary, or in a heronry among those of many great blues, or even among the nests of other species of wading birds. The great blue usually builds its nest in the highest portion of the foliage, whether in tall pines or in low-growing mangroves. Great blues may build their nests on the ground where little vegetation is available, such as on cliffs on the West Coast. Nesting areas may be used by herons for many years. Once a female has been attracted, the birds go through a series of spectacular courtship displays or "morning love dances." One such maneuver, the head-down display—which includes erection of the crest and neck feathers and downward thrusts of the head—is also used as a territorial defense against other herons when sitting on the nest; the pair may also cross necks at this time. Preening may occur when one of the birds rubs its bill gently over its mate's back, head, or neck. Swaying is another courtship display, during which the pair lock the tips of their bills and then sway back and forth together. Courtship generally continues throughout the entire nesting period.

Great blues do not breed until their second or third year of age. Copulation usually occurs near or on the nest. The female first lowers her body with her head flat against the nest, and then the male climbs on her back with his wings flapping for stabilization. He may also grasp her neck with his beak while mating.

Since some nests are used over and over, material is added every year, and eventually the nests become quite substantial in size. Sometimes the birds rob old nest sites (or even active ones) of twigs while reconstructing new sites. The male collects twigs about one foot long and anywhere from one-quarter to one-half inch in diameter, then passes them off to the female, which does the actual nest building. Many nests are lined with marsh grasses, willow leaves, pine needles, or, in the South, Spanish moss. The female greets the stick-carrying male each time he comes with a stretch display before he hands off his twig.

The female great blue lays her eggs every two days until her clutch reaches four eggs. The eggs are bluish green, approximately 64 x 45mm. Both parents share the twenty-eight-day incubation duties, turning the eggs with their beaks approximately every two hours. It is reported that great blues have only one brood in a nesting season, but I have witnessed a great blue parent standing at the edge of one nest and feeding eight-week-old young and then flying to a second nest to incubate eggs. This occurred at the Venice, Florida, heronry in the spring of 1992.

When the chicks first hatch, they can do little but crawl around the nest. The adults at this time regurgitate a fairly well-digested meal of fish, amphibians, or reptiles into the nest, then pick up the bits in their beaks and place the food in the chicks' mouths. The young have large heads for their body size and are covered by a grayish down. Since the chicks hatch out approximately every two days, the older chicks are more likely to survive—especially during periods when less food is available. Often these older chicks are more aggressive and consume more of the food; at times, they will even peck their younger siblings. Fewer than 50 percent of great blue herons survive their first year. The young, whose feathers develop early on, lie flat in their nest until they recognize their parents. They'll then stand up excitedly and call an *ak-ak-ak-ak* until they are fed or until they lose sight of the adults.

Soon, the parents regurgitate larger chunks of food into their own beaks, allowing the young to ram their beaks in—usually crosswise—to obtain food. Sometimes several birds try to grab a parent's beak, simultaneously jerking the adult so violently that it may leave the nest for a while before returning to resume feeding all over again.

As the young mature, the adults may regurgitate the whole fish into the nest and allow the young to eat while they fly off in search of more food. At the age of approximately seven to eight weeks, the young will leave the nest, staying close to their parents for another three weeks while the adults still feed them. After this time, the young disperse and begin to feed together.

Great blues spend as much as 90 percent of their time feeding in and around water. They stand motionless for long periods of time, waiting until a fish or small turtle swims within striking range. With neck outstretched, the four-foot bird can watch over a large area. They usually walk slowly and deliberately, so as not to disturb the water's surface, until jabbing swiftly at potential prey. When a great blue catches small fish, it usually doesn't stab at the fish but, rather, catches it sideways in its bill, then flips it in the air, and swallows. The bird generally first spears larger fish, then takes them to shore. There the great blue stabs the fish repeatedly and then grabs it and flips it up head first before swallowing it. Great blues have been known to chase other birds, especially cormorants and anhingas in the Everglades, and rob them of their prey. Larger herons have also been known to swim after fish going into deeper waters. Most feeding is done in the daytime, but it is not uncommon for herons to also feed at night.

The voice of the great blue is a deep croak emitted when the bird is alarmed or defending its territory, which is vast. This species is the most widespread of all North

OPPOSITE TOP: *Twig passing is part of the complex bonding behavior exhibited by a mated pair of great blue herons.* OPPOSITE BOTTOM RIGHT: *A fledgling heron grasps its parent's beak, which will open slightly and dump partially digested chunks of food down its throat.*

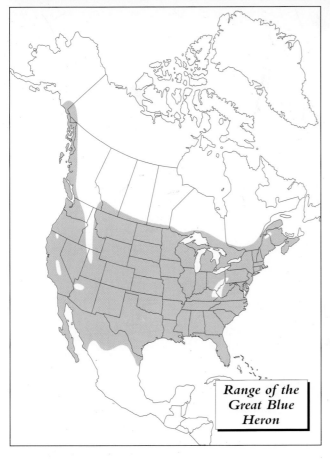

Range of the
Great Blue
Heron

American herons, nesting from southern Alaska to the equator. Many in the South move from only one local area to another as their food supply shifts, but the majority migrate, sometimes alone, other times in flocks of six to thirty. Spring migration begins in February and runs through May for birds flying farther north; fall migration begins in mid-September and runs through October.

Horicon Marsh Wildlife Area and Horicon National Wildlife Refuge

Horicon Marsh in southeastern Wisconsin encompasses the 20,976 acres of the Horicon National Wildlife Refuge and the 10,962 acres of the Horicon Marsh Wildlife Area. Horicon Marsh is the largest freshwater cattail marsh in the nation, making the wetlands a natural home to 248 different bird species. Many migratory birds use Horicon as a staging ground for trips southward.

Fourmile Island in the southern portion of the marsh is home to a total of over a thousand nesting pairs of great blue herons, black-crowned night-herons, and great egrets. The island is designated as a State Natural Area due to its remarkable wading bird population, and it is the only one of the 227 flora-oriented Natural Areas in Wisconsin set aside specifically for the wildlife population. As this is the northland, these magnificent birds head south in the winter, but during the rest of the year, viewing the abundant herons and egrets on Fourmile Island is easy.

The Department of Natural Resources offers weekend-long naturalist programs every spring and fall. Group tours and guided hikes are available throughout the year, though they need to be set up ahead of time. Contact the area's Wildlife Naturalist for more information. Outside of the few closed areas in the Refuge and Wildlife Area, canoeing and hiking are encouraged. Canoe rentals are available in the town of Horicon.

The Horicon National Wildlife Refuge and the Horicon Marsh Wildlife Area are located almost dead center in a triangle created by Green Bay, Madison, and Milwaukee. East of the town of Beaver Dam on State Highway 33, the town of Horicon forms the base of the wildlife area. North Palmatory Street will take you from the town to the state DNR headquarters inside Horicon Marsh.

Wisconsin Department of Natural Resources
Horicon Area Headquarters
N7725 Highway 28
Horicon, WI 53032-9782
(414) 387-7873

OPPOSITE: *A row of great blue heron nests built of large twigs lines the banks of Rabbit Island, just off the coast of Louisiana. Ground nesting by herons and egrets usually occurs when there are no predators.* ABOVE: *Young great blues, now as large as their parents, hang their wings open to dissipate heat while standing alert and watching for their next meal.* OVERLEAF: *After the great blue heron young are several weeks old, the parent may drop whole fish directly into the nest rather than first swallowing them before returning to the nest.*

Great White Heron
ARDEA HERODIAS OCCIDENTALIS

The great white heron is not a separate species but, rather, a white morph of the great blue heron, not unlike the white morphs of the reddish egret. The bird is solid white and stands approximately fifty-one inches tall with an eighty-inch wingspan. It has a large yellow beak as well as distinct yellow legs, which distinguish the bird from the slightly smaller and trimmer great egret, which has black legs. The irides (irises) are also yellow, and the lores are blue, sometimes with a tinge of green. ● Great whites are almost exclusively saltwater feeders that wade the shallows to catch fish, crab, and shrimp, although some do wander into the interior of the Everglades in summer. They prefer to make their nests in red and black mangroves. A rather large heronry is located about midway down and slightly west of the Florida Keys in the Great White Heron Refuge. These small islands also have thousands of double-crested cormorants interspersed with the herons. ● Great whites are the most restricted in range of any North American heron, found from the Florida Keys to Tampa Bay. The great white heron also ranges south to Cuba, along the coasts of the Yucatan and possibly the islands off the northern coast of Venezuela. While most of the great white herons' nesting occurs in winter and spring, some pairs seem to nest at all times of the year, with the fewest nesting between August and October. A few mixed nestings with the blue form and white form have been sighted in Florida Bay, but they are not very common.

Since the great white heron occurs only in southern Florida, it has had to adapt to the large human population. Great white herons raid unattended campsites along Florida Bay, and they sometimes scatter gear all about in search of food. Many birds stand around nearby piers waiting for local fishermen to throw out the entrails of fish after cleaning them.

Range of the
Great White
Heron

RIGHT: *Poor water management practices in the Everglades have caused the loss of much of the former feeding habitat for many wading birds, resulting in a sharp reduction in the number of wading birds that nest in this region.*

Everglades National Park

Southern Florida's Everglades National Park is close to 1.6 million acres of sawgrass, pine forest, hammocks, and mangrove estuaries. This reserve—a biosphere of international importance—contains a significant portion of the largest sawgrass marsh in the world. Visitors drive the thirty-eight-mile paved road that ends at Flamingo in search of wading birds. Although the park is open year-round, the best wading bird observations occur during the dry season between November and May.

The first area for viewing egrets and herons after entering the park is located at the Royal Palm Visitor Center

on the Anhinga Trail. Great egrets, great blue herons, snowy egrets, green-backed herons, and, of course, anhingas all forage here—and several pairs of anhinga nest here in some years.

Paurotis Pond is an area best visited about an hour before sunset, when large flocks of white ibises soar low overhead as they prepare to roost on an island in the pond.

Although a number of small lakes can be glimpsed from the road, the next best area for viewing wading birds is Mrazek Pond. The best time to arrive is just before sunrise. During the winter months, the pond's water level drops (unless there are unseasonal rains); when the level reaches a certain point, birds flock here from all over. It is

not uncommon to see several hundred birds feeding here at the same time. This happens only once or twice during the season and may last for only a few days. Even so, smaller numbers of birds still feed here in the early morning.

Eco Pond, located on the right-hand side of the road in Flamingo, between the cabins and campground, has been overgrown in part by a tremendous stand of cattails. From an elevated platform, visitors may view roseate spoonbills, snowy egrets, white ibises, and great egrets roosting on a central island. Large numbers of wading birds are often seen along the Shark Valley Tram road at the north end of the park, accessible from U.S. 41 (the Tamiami Trail).

A number of interpretive programs are available throughout the Everglades National Park. To reach the park from Homestead, Florida, travel southwest on Highway 9336 and follow the park's signs until you come to the entrance.

Superintendent
Everglades National Park
40001 State Road 9336
Homestead, FL 33034-6733
(305) 242-7700

Great Egret
CASMERODIUS ALBUS

The great egret is one of North America's most graceful wading birds. Standing at a height of thirty-seven to forty-one inches, with a wingspan of four and one-half feet, this slender white bird can be distinguished from the white phase of the great blue heron by the kink in its long, slender neck and its black legs. The great egret's irises are yellow, and its bill is yellow with a black line from the gape to beyond the eye. The lores are yellow except during courtship, when they turn a brilliant green. During the breeding period, the great egret grows approximately thirty-five aigrettes, long, flowing plumes that extend from the back and trail almost a foot beyond its tail. Noted ornithologist Arthur C. Bent, in his 1926 volume about marsh birds, compares the graceful plumes to "a bridal train." The egret's legs and feet are customarily black, although during the mating season the upper part of the tibia turns a salmon color. By summer, the long aigrettes are usually worn down, at which time they are shed. ● During courtship, the male elevates his large, showy plumes, sometimes with a slight quiver. The male egret's voice is usually a coarse, raspy *krawk,* but during courtship he emits a soft gurgling sound. To attract his mate, he uses circle flights and employs his "advertisement" call. ● The male great egret defends his nesting territory from other males first with upright displays, then with arched neck and forward displays. I have observed great egrets during the mating season at the Venice, Florida, rookery battle in the air just above the nest sites. With wings outstretched, they jab their bills and kick at one another with their long legs and feet, all the while emitting loud, coarse calls. ● After the female accepts a mate, the male continues to display for another six days; after each display, the pair mates. Mock preening and allo-preening occur after the couple bond. The male selects the nest site, generally preferring a site above water. The birds may nest at heights from three to fifty feet, but in mixed colonies they tend to nest higher than the smaller species. In my observations,

The great egret performs the stretch display of its courtship ritual by first pointing its bill skyward, then thrusting its head downward. Its long aigrettes are erected during this activity. The great egret's green lores show that it is in breeding plumage.

PREVIOUS PAGES: *Early morning finds dozens of egrets standing motionless, watching for prey to come within striking range. The birds fly in about a half hour before sunrise.* ABOVE: *A great egret prepares to land in its heronry. It has to be accurate, since landing in another bird's territory will trigger a flapping confrontation.* RIGHT: *The great egret's long aigrettes will become ragged, and eventually the bird will molt the beautiful plumes. Its green lores have already faded, turning back to yellow.*

the great egret nests earlier than the smaller birds and a bit later than the great blues. Great egrets have also been observed nesting with large colonies of wood storks. Great egrets construct their nests of coarse sticks; the female builds or reconstructs old nests while the male gathers the sticks. Each time a stick is passed, the male and female go through a greeting ceremony of plume and wing raising. In Louisiana and northwest Tennessee, great egrets prefer cypress trees for nesting; along the Gulf Coast, nests are built on islands in the tops of low-growing shrubs and mangroves. On the Texas coast, nests can be found in patches of cacti.

The egrets produce one brood in a season, laying three or four pale bluish eggs approximately 57 x 41mm. Both sexes incubate the eggs, but the female is thought to be the primary incubator, especially at night. Great egrets line their nests with willow leaves, grasses, and mangrove leaves and do not hesitate to steal twigs from the nests of neighboring tricolored herons. They may lay eggs as early as December in the South and as late as July in their extreme northern range. Incubation occurs for about twenty-three to twenty-four days, after which time the young birds crawl helplessly around the nest. The young are covered with white down and have yellow beaks and straw-colored eyes. Both parents feed the chicks at this time, regurgitating food into the nest and then picking up bits to place in the babies' mouths. Two or three young may be fed in a single feeding. The two largest and most aggressive chicks often will give their younger, smaller siblings a fatal jab with their sharp bills to eliminate competition for food.

At about three weeks, young egrets begin to emerge from their nest and flap their wings—a behavior encouraged by the parent, which lands a few yards away from the nest with the food. Once the chick spots its parent, it loudly *krawks* or *kaks* in repetition (a habit of many other young wading birds). The young even participate in a ritual in which they appear to be feeding one another, which, of course, they are not. After the parent's arrival at the nest site, it regurgitates food into its own beak, allowing the young to thrust their beaks in to grab their meals. By the age of approximately fourteen months, the young have attained their full adult plumage.

The egret is a diurnal feeder and prefers to feed in tidal marshes, swamps, and the fringes of open water. Fish are the mainstay of its diet, but it also eats frogs, crayfish, crabs, lizards, insects, fruits, seeds, and other vegetation. The great egret will stand quietly, waiting for prey to come within striking range, although 60 to 90 percent of its time is spent walking slowly and feeding. While wading in shallow water, the egret will tilt its head to spot prey.

Pulling its head back, the egret jabs at lightning speed, grabbing small fish in its beak or impaling larger fish. After catching larger fish, the egret may go ashore to stab the fish a few more times or to beat it against the ground. It then grabs the fish in its beak, flips it head first, and swallows it. On one occasion, I observed a great egret attempting to grasp a slippery catfish in its beak and flip it. The entire process took well over thirty minutes, because every time the egret got the fish in its beak and began to lift its head, the fish would slip out and fall to the ground. Great egrets are fairly solitary when feeding, unless prey is unusually abundant. Mrazek Pond in the Everglades National Park is a good example of a site where group feeding often takes place. When the water level drops in the dry season between November and May, more prey are concentrated in this small area. In fact, I have counted more than one hundred great egrets feeding together. Mixed among the egrets were spoonbills, snowy egrets, tricoloreds, wood storks, and white ibises. During periods when food is less abundant, great egrets vigorously defend their territory, principally from their own species, while occasionally robbing smaller waders of their catches.

The great egret is one of the most cosmopolitan of herons: Its northeastern population migrates along the Atlantic Coast region to the Bahamas and Antilles, while the midwestern population winters in Florida. The western group moves down to Mexico and Central America.

Venice Florida Rookery

There are hundreds of city parks in the Southeast with small nesting colonies of wading birds. One of my favorites is located in Venice, Florida, a town of about fifteen thousand on the Gulf of Mexico coast. This small, three-acre park behind the Florida Highway Patrol headquarters building is host to nesting great blue herons, great egrets, snowy egrets, anhingas, black-crowned night-herons, and cattle egrets. While nesting occurs almost any month of the year, the birds seem to be more active February through May. The birds nest on a small island no more than thirty yards from shore; alligators in the pond keep the area predator-free.

Photographers and birders line the nearby grassy shoreline, but the birds ignore them while going about their courtship, nesting, and raising of young. Great blue herons have been known to attempt to steal cable releases for their nesting material from photographic gear left unattended. Near sunset, the population quadruples in size as birds fly in to roost for the night. Visitors park along the

side of the road and walk no more than twenty-five to thirty-five yards to the pond's edge. Pine trees provide shade for those watching the birds at midday.

From I-75 take the Venice, Jacaranda Boulevard exit. When Jacaranda intersects Highway 41, turn right, and immediately on the left is the Highway Patrol headquarters. Turn down the small street that leads behind the headquarters, and on the right side you will see the nesting area.

(no address)

ABOVE: *Strong winds blow up this egret's showy "bridal train." Like the snowy egret, the great egret was once widely hunted for its magnificent feathers.*

Range of the Great Egret

ABOVE: *Egrets congregate on a small island for the evening. Some islands host thousands of birds roosting overnight.* LEFT: *Water sprays as a great egret stabs at a small fish. These birds rarely miss, due to their quickness.*

The long filamentous aigrettes—the lacy plumes on the bird's back—exhibited by snowy egrets during courtship were prized during the nineteenth century by millinery trade, causing the near-extinction of these birds. Ornithologist John James Audubon once remarked, after shooting into the birds' nests, that there seemed to be fewer egrets to collect than a few years earlier. During courtship, the snowy egret's lores—located between the beak and eyes—turn red or reddish orange, as do the normally yellow feet.

Snowy Egret
EGRETTA THULA

The snowy egret is perhaps the most beautiful of all herons, its delicacy emphasized by magnificent sweeping plumes that curve beyond its tail feathers. The snowy stands approximately two feet tall with a wingspan of thirty-eight inches. Its plumage is always a solid white, with yellow lores and yellow irides. Distinguishing the snowy from other waders are its narrow black bill, solid black legs in adults, and bright yellow feet. The immature snowy egret, which exhibits a yellow stripe up the back of its legs, does not acquire full adult plumage until approximately eighteen months. ● The snowy is confused at times with the cattle egret, a stouter bird with a yellowish bill that lacks the yellow feet of the snowy, and with the white immature little blue heron. The adult snowy always has a crest of feathers on its head, which it erects when excited. During high breeding, its lores become pinkish red and its feet turn red to orangish red. This is the only accurate way to determine high breeding. ● During courtship, snowy egrets grow long, filamentous plumes that extend down the back and curve up near the tail. After the male selects a territory, he begins to advertise with circle and tumble flights. While exhibiting the stretch display (the most common among these birds), the male becomes very vocal, calling *wah-wah-wah*. This stretch display is usually far more elaborate in the snowy than among other egrets. Pointing his bill skyward, the male pumps his head up and down. ● The male snowy defends his nesting territory aggressively and chases off intruders with loud squawks. While both sexes display the extraordinary pure-white plumes, it is the male which marches back and forth in front of the female. With crest raised, lower neck feathers spread, and breast feathers pushed out, the male soon wins the attention of his prospective mate. ● Snowies prefer nesting near or over open water and are found in mixed colonies of other wading birds. Like all herons, the male and female snowy construct their nest together—the male bringing twigs to his mate. The nests, which are lined with leaves, reeds, and other soft materials, are usually built in shrubs or on lower branches of trees no higher than ten feet off the ground. The female lays four or five greenish blue eggs approximately 43 x 32mm and produces but one brood in a season.

Predatory fish crows, snakes, and raccoons are this bird's major enemies. In St. Augustine, Florida, where snowy egrets nest in the middle of the alligator swamp exhibit at the Alligator Farm, only crows have been able to affect the colony, since no terrestrial animals can make it past the giant reptiles. In early May 1992, crows raided this nesting colony and took the birds' eggs. The snowies then abandoned their nests for approximately a week before resuming courtship all over again and renesting.

Since eggs are laid approximately every two days, the last chick to hatch may be a full week younger than the first hatchling. Unless food is plentiful, the youngest will most certainly not survive, due to the aggressive nature of the older and larger siblings.

Young birds are covered with white down, and the bare portions of their skin are green. The bill and feet are yellow. During their first week, the helpless young birds must be fed by a parent, which places regurgitated bits of food directly into the babies' mouths. Nestlings this young must be shaded from the hot sun and protected from rain by an adult. Once the young are feathered, they are less bothered by the elements. At approximately three weeks of age, young snowies climb out onto limbs near their nests — a behavior encouraged by parents, which stand off the nest for long periods. Unfortunately, this activity can result in mortality for the young if they lose their footing and drop to the ground or water, where predators may be lurking.

At the age of six weeks, the young leave the nest. Unlike the great egret, the snowy egret usually flies in flocks, displaying faster wing beats. After reaching its destination, the snowy drops in fast, nearly tumbling to the ground.

Snowy egrets are diurnal feeders and employ a wide range of feeding techniques. One effective behavior for catching small prey is foot stirring and foot raking, which scares up small fish and crustaceans that the snowy grabs as it strikes forward with its sharp beak. On other occasions, the snowy may hover before dipping down to drop its feet in the water. This technique moves the prey in front of the bird before it seizes its victim.

Perhaps the most unusual of all its feeding behaviors is bill vibrating. Crouching over the water with its neck pulled slightly back, the snowy places its bill in contact with the water surface and begins to vibrate its bill. This sets up ripples in the water that attract small fish searching for prey that has dropped to the water. Once within range, the unsuspecting fish are grabbed by the egret. Another feeding behavior — usually associated only with the cattle egret — involves following livestock to catch insects. Some of the snowy egret's other food includes cutworms, frogs, crabs, and mollusks.

The breeding range in the United States is along the Atlantic Coast from Maine to Florida; from Florida to Texas on the Gulf of Mexico; on California's Pacific Coast; and in interiors north to Nevada, southern Idaho, South Dakota, and Kansas. Most nesting takes place around the coastal areas, although snowies often nest inland in smaller numbers. Like those of other egrets, regional populations of snowy egrets migrate into different areas. The mid-Atlantic population migrates to Florida, the Caribbean, and into northern South America, while the western group ends up in Mexico. The mid-continental flocks migrate to Central America, and the Florida birds may spend their winter in Panama.

St. Augustine's Alligator Farm

The Alligator Farm in St. Augustine, Florida, is perhaps the last place you'd expect to find nesting wading birds. But birds have nested at the farm for more than forty years. Visitors will probably never be able to stand closer to nesting egrets and herons than along these wooden boardwalks. The staff continually trims back tree limbs, since the birds would nest over the boardwalk if given the chance. Tricolored herons, great egrets, snowy egrets, green-backed herons, and cattle egrets all nest here from March through June every year. May is probably the best month to observe the most species of birds.

Like the Venice Rookery, also in Florida, it is the alligators — in this case, hundreds of alligators — that protect the birds from predators, such as raccoons. Unfortunately, from time to time crows raid the snowy egrets' and tricolored herons' nests of eggs, but the farm's staff is quick to harass the crows into eventually leaving. The egrets and herons will then exhibit courtship behavior and nest again.

The Alligator Farm is located on A1A, just south of downtown St. Augustine.

St. Augustine's Alligator Farm
Route A1A
St. Augustine, FL 32084
(904) 824-3337

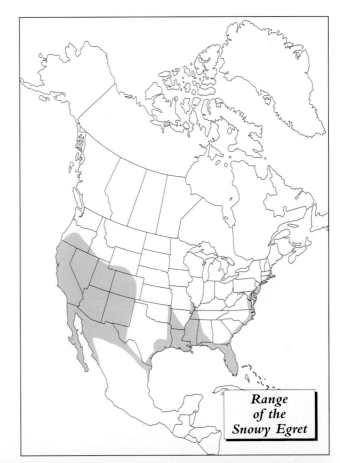

BELOW: *Egrets and herons find areas surrounded by alligators to be ideal nesting sites, since alligators keep out the birds' chief predator, the raccoon. Occasionally young snowies fall into the water or adults nest too low, but these are the only times the large reptiles pose a threat to the birds.*

ABOVE: *After courtship and nesting have begun, the snowy egret's lores and feet return to their normal yellow color.* INSET LEFT: *The snowy egret grabs smaller prey with its beak and impales larger animals.*

INSET TOP: *A snowy egret grasps the bill of a parent while receiving regurgitated fish caught from the nearby Intracoastal Waterway.* ABOVE: *Snowies usually fly in small flocks that range in size from ten to twenty birds. Their heads are pulled back on their shoulders, and their yellow feet trail out behind their tails.*

A little blue heron pursues a small fish through waters of Taylor Slough in Everglades National Park. These birds usually are solitary when feeding, although group feeding occurs where food is abundant.

Little Blue Heron

EGRETTA CAERULEA

Like the tricolored heron, the little blue heron is not endowed with long aigrettes or showy plumage. It is stockier than the tricolored heron, between twenty-four and twenty-eight inches tall, with a forty-inch wingspan. The little blue has a long neck that it rarely pulls in when resting, which makes the bird seem always alert. Its coloring is dark blue-gray all over. The slender bill is bluish gray except for the tip, which is blacker. The irides are yellow, and the legs and feet are olive gray. ● During breeding season, the little blue heron's irides change to brownish gray, and its legs and feet turn black. The now obviously bicolored bill becomes a bright blue, like the lores, at the base and black on the tip. A few dark head plumes develop, and the head and neck take on a strong purplish cast. ● Little blue herons usually travel in small flocks with their heads pulled in on their shoulders. Although little blues nest in coastal colonies, the larger nesting colonies are in freshwater habitats, which may account for the large breeding population in the Atchafalaya Swamp not far from New Orleans in Louisiana. Little blues are more likely to pick an island area for nesting than are other herons. When nesting inland in smaller colonies, little blues often prefer willow thickets. ● The male begins the courtship process by selecting a vantage point from which he can be seen as he begins stretch displays (exhibited only by males). He starts by bowing, with the feathers on his neck extended and swaying. He moves toward the female until they come together and start bill clapping and rubbing their necks together. At this time they copulate; then they begin to build the nest. While the male presents his mate with nesting twigs, the pair spread their wings in a greeting ceremony and may copulate several more times. ● Little blue herons prefer to nest in dense growth, usually three to ten feet high. The nests, which are not tightly constructed and use less building material than those of many other herons, will contain four or five bluish green eggs, approximately 44 x 34mm. The eggs require a little over three weeks of incubation, customarily shared by both sexes. An unusual occurrence of egg carrying was observed by James A. Rodgers Jr., who concluded that the bird, which was taking one egg at a time in its bill, was moving them to another nest. Like most other herons, the little blue heron staggers its hatchings. What surprises the casual observer of the little blue is the discovery that chicks are covered in solid white down.

After the eggs hatch, one parent at a time goes off to seek food, while the other protects the young from would-be predators and shields them from heat or damp. As time goes by, both parents begin to look for food at the same time, returning to regurgitate the partially digested crayfish, frogs, fish, and mollusks. The young often jerk violently when probing the adults' bills with their own—so much so that it is a wonder the parents are not lacerated.

Juvenile birds are solid white except for their black-tipped primaries, which are hard to see. In their second year, little blues start a transitional period, during which they get blotches of blue feathers, and their plumage is termed "calico" or "pied." These birds may breed before molting into their slate-blue adult plumage. Their coloration is considered unique among the herons.

Little blues are not night feeders. Instead, they prefer early morning or evening feeding, generally alone or in small groups. Some biologists have suggested that the little blue heron exhibits individual feeding specialization. What this means is that a particular heron may learn how to catch frogs successfully, so this becomes its primary prey. Other scientists argue, however, that specific birds choose a favorite location where one type of prey just happens to be more abundant. In the Corkscrew Swamp Sanctuary, for example, there was a particular little blue heron that fished around the water lettuce pond for a number of years. This bird would walk on top of the floating vegetation with its large feet, pulling the plants back and seeking frogs, mollusks, and small fish. The little blue also will follow along after grazing cattle, catching insects in the same manner as the cattle egret.

The little blue heron can be found throughout Florida up the Atlantic Coast to Maryland and Massachusetts. It occurs in large numbers in the southern part of the Mississippi River valley and the Gulf Coast into Texas, and also in South America, Peru, and the West Indies.

J. N. "Ding" Darling National Wildlife Refuge

Located on Florida's Sanibel Island, the J. N. "Ding" Darling National Wildlife Refuge—5,014 acres of water and mangroves—supports magnificent displays of almost every species of wading birds. Wildlife- and bird-watchers follow a one-way, five-mile road built on top of dikes originally constructed for mosquito control. To see the most wildlife, visitors should arrive at sunrise just as the refuge opens its gate. The roadbed is as wide as any other Florida highway, so if you spot an interesting animal, you can pull over without blocking traffic.

The road runs along a canal where anhingas perch in mangroves, drying their wings. On each side of the road are areas open to wide expanses of water. Great egrets, reddish egrets, roseate spoonbills, white ibises, little blue herons, wood storks, and many other species can be seen wading and feeding. Early morning is the best time for viewing, especially when low tide coincides with sunrise. Evening also has a fairly sizable concentration of birds before they return to their night roosts.

Refuge headquarters house permanent exhibits as well as slide and video interpretive programs. There is also a large bookstore and a helpful volunteer staff in the facility.

While most visitation occurs from January through March, I have found large numbers of wading birds, especially roseate spoonbills, in May—though they usually disperse by about 9:00 A.M.

From Fort Myers, drive west to the Sanibel Causeway, where you will have to pay a toll. Continue on until you come to a stop sign, turn right on Periwinkle Way, proceed to the end, and make a right turn onto Tarpon Bay Road. Proceed to the four-way stop and turn left on Sanibel-Captiva Road. The refuge is well marked and will be approximately two miles on the right.

J. N. "Ding" Darling National Wildlife Refuge
1 Wildlife Drive
Sanibel, FL 33957
(813) 472-1100

OPPOSITE TOP RIGHT: *In its breeding plumage, a little blue heron walks across floating water lettuce in search of crayfish, snails, frogs, and other prey. Occasionally a little blue missteps and falls through, only to recover by flying a short distance and landing on a more stable mass of floating vegetation.* OPPOSITE BOTTOM: *This young heron is acquiring its adult blue feathers. During this phase, it is referred to as pied or calico. Peering is a feeding technique that involves standing motionless and gazing into the water until prey like this small fish comes into striking range.*

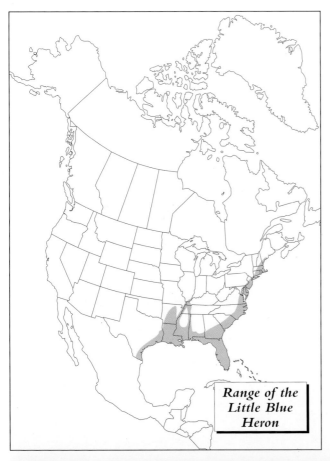

Range of the Little Blue Heron

ABOVE: *Except when the birds are copulating, the only way to tell a male tricolored heron from a female is by observing the male present its mate with a nesting twig.* IN-SET: *The white underfeathers signal to observers that it is a tricolored heron preparing to mate. Wings are used for balance when the male climbs on top of the female. The male tricolored heron will grasp the female's shoulders to copulate. These birds will mate numerous times throughout nest building.*

Tricolored Heron
Egretta tricolor

This thin, graceful bird is one of the more common herons in the South. Once referred to as the Louisiana heron, the tricolored heron stands approximately twenty-eight inches tall with a wingspan of three feet. This wading bird is an unmistakable dark slate-blue with white undersides. A line of white and brown runs down its entire neck, from chin to breast, and its back and irides are brownish yellow. The tricolored is confused at times with the little blue heron, which lacks the white undersides and neck coloring. The sexes look alike, although the male is slightly larger. "For harmony in colors and for grace in motion," the distinguished ornithologist Arthur C. Bent declared nearly ninety years ago, "this little heron has few rivals." ● During breeding season, the tricolored's irides turn a brilliant red and its lores a magnificent blue. The bird's bill at this time also turns blue with a black tip, and its legs turn pinkish red. A few pure white head plumes develop at this time, and the neck feathers turn purplish. The tricolored's back feathers reveal a slightly golden tinge. ● During courtship, the male selects a nest site, constructs a loose pile of twigs, and then begins to exhibit the characteristic snap and stretch display. Standing on or near the nesting spot, he pulls his head back on his shoulders and points his slender neck skyward. After thrusting his head upward, he reaches downward without hesitation, grabs a twig, and gently shakes it. The male also makes a low vocal noise during courtship, which in turn seems to make the female more receptive. The male and female continue to copulate during nest building and the greeting ceremony, when the male presents his mate with a twig and displays outstretched wings and a raised crest. ● Since tricolored herons are colonial nesters, conflicts arise among the different species. They often jab at one another in a threatening display, but few fights actually break out. If one lands too near another's nest, the nesting bird usually flies toward the intruder. This action is usually enough to displace the unwanted bird. ● After the female com-

OPPOSITE: *The incubating heron parent periodically stands off the eggs in order to turn them.*
RIGHT TOP: *At this point in the age of the young, the tricolored parent places bits of regurgitated food in the babies' mouths. In another week, the young will grab the adult's bill, causing the parent to regurgitate directly into their beaks. An unhatched egg may stay in an active nest until the young tricolored herons have fledged. In many cases, however, the egg is crushed or knocked out.*
RIGHT MIDDLE: *Two young tricolored herons sit waiting for their parents to return with food. It is easy to see how these young birds can swallow large prey, from the size of their large mouths.*
RIGHT BOTTOM: *Tricolored herons feed by stabbing or seizing fish, crayfish (pictured), amphibians, crustaceans, and insects.*

pletes the nest, which is usually no more than ten feet off the ground and often over water, she lays three or four greenish blue eggs, which she and her mate incubate for about twenty-one days. The female usually incubates during the night, while the male roosts on a limb next to the nest. The approximate size of the heron's egg is 45 x 33mm, roughly the same as the snowy egret's. Unless you see a tricolored land on the nest, you can't be sure whether the eggs you have discovered belong to the heron or to a snowy egret. I have photographed nests with greenish blue eggs in tall grasses when I was unable to wait and watch from a distance to see what bird would return to the nest; I still do not know which species of egg I photographed.

During incubation, the parent bird turns the egg gently with its long, slender bill. While still inside the egg, the chick begins to peck, creating a small hole in the shell. At this time, the adult may stand up in the nest. After the little bird slowly cracks open the egg and wriggles from the broken shell, the parent ejects the shell from the nest. Because herons stagger their egg laying, the hatching process may take as long as a week. Some eggs do not hatch at all, and on one particular nest I recall an egg was left undisturbed all the way to the other young bird's fledging.

Like most other herons, the parents first regurgitate the food into the nest during early development and place bits of food into their babies' mouths. On hot sunny days and rainy days, parents shield their young by partially extending their wings to serve as a canopy.

Early on, the chicks are covered with gray down. At about three weeks they begin to climb from the nest, balancing themselves clumsily on the limbs that support their nesting platform. Upon seeing their parent return with food, the young become quite noisy and in their excitement may start pecking at one another. At the age of five weeks, the young leave the nest but return to trees around the colony to be fed by the adults. By this time their long necks have turned a reddish brown. They will not attain their adult plumage, however, until about sixteen months.

Tricolored herons prefer habitats that have shallow marshes, mud flats, and swamps. They also nest on oyster reef islands around the Louisiana-Texas coast. They are hailed by many as an economic benefit, since they eat crayfish that inhabit flooded rice fields.

Tricoloreds feed in brackish saltwater and in fresh water, usually wading alone and stabbing or seizing fish, crayfish, amphibians, crustaceans, and insects. "Not a snail can escape its keen search," John James Audubon wrote in 1840, "and as it moves around the muddy pool, it secures each water lizard that occurs. . . ." These waders employ a variety of techniques to feed, including foot stirring and raking, hopping, and walking slowly. The tricolored also "canopy-feeds," extending its wings to form an umbrella that reduces the sun's glare and produces a shaded area attractive to potential prey. The tricolored is often found feeding with the little pied-billed grebe, a diving bird that is believed to drive fish and other prey toward the heron.

The North American nesting range of this heron is from the coast of Maine all the way to the coast of Texas. It is found throughout the southern states and occurs along both coasts of Mexico down into Central and South America. Generally, the tricolored is much more common along coasts than inland, but it does nest in large numbers in some interior Everglades colonies and often nests in association with snowy egrets. Some ornithologists suggest the reason the tricolored is so abundant today is that it was not hunted by plume hunters at the turn of the century. Men and women concerned about fashion seemed to favor the white filamentous aigrettes of the snowy and great egret for their hats and the pink feathers of the roseate spoonbill for their fans.

Laguna Atascosa National Wildlife Refuge

This 45,187-acre Texas sanctuary is the southernmost refuge in the United States. Sheltered by Padre Island, Laguna Atascosa consists of estuaries, marshes, ponds, tropical mangroves, yucca, and prickly pear. A slight elevation change creates savannas and habitat for thornbush and mesquite. The fifteen-mile bayside road carries visitors first through brushy areas, along the seashore and through coastal prairie. Redhead Ridge Overlook affords the visitor a better view of the Laguna Madre and a small lake.

The second refuge road is the two-mile lakeside tour, which leads past channels that were at one time flooded by the Rio Grande and Laguna Atascosa Lake. Reddish egrets, tricolored herons, snowy egrets, little blue herons, and spoonbills can be seen between Laguna Madre and the Padre Island National Seashore. As in most other Texas coastal areas, wading birds are quite abundant here throughout much of the year, and waterfowl winter here as well.

From Harlingen, Texas, go east twenty-five miles on FM 106; refuge signs will direct you north on Buena Vista Road for approximately three miles to the headquarters.

Laguna Atascosa National Wildlife Refuge
P.O. Box 450
Rio Hono, TX 78583
(210) 748-3607

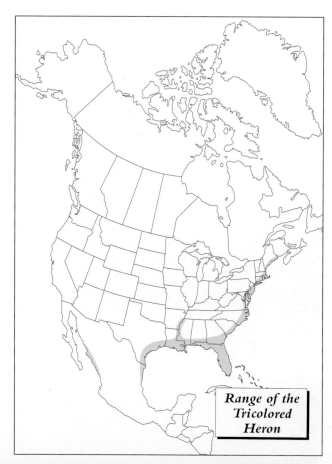

Range of the Tricolored Heron

BELOW: *The golden color on its back and long white head plumes indicate this tricolored heron is sporting its breeding plumage. At this stage of nesting it has lost its brilliant red irides and blue and black bill.*

ABOVE: *The white phase of the reddish egret has the same range as the dark, or colored, phase, although a higher percentage of whites are found in the Texas population than in the Florida group.* INSET: *The strongly bicolored bill is one of the field marks that help bird-watchers to identify the reddish egret. These birds prefer shallow tidal flats along the Gulf Coast.*

Reddish Egret
EGRETTA RUFESCENS

Highly sensitive to environmental change, especially habitat loss due to heavy development along the Gulf Coast, the reddish egret is the rarest heron in North America. It stands approximately thirty inches tall with a wingspan of three and one-half feet. The adult reddish egret's head and neck are a chestnut color; its neck, breast, and crown are covered with lanceolate, or tapered, plumes. The body is a neutral gray, and the eyes are straw-colored. The female is slightly smaller than the male. ● The reddish egret is dichromorphic—that is, it exhibits two color phases. The colored phase, sometimes called the dark phase, is seen in Texas and Florida; the coloring of these birds is sometimes confused with the plumage of the smaller little blue heron. The pure white color phase is distributed irregularly and is often confused with the snowy egret. However, the differentiation between the pure white phase and the snowy is first apparent in the beak, which, in the reddish egret, is strongly bicolored. Other differences are apparent, too: The reddish egret's white morph does not have black legs and yellow feet like the snowy egret, and its tibia are flesh-colored and its toes are dark green. ● A pinkish flesh-color and black hue cover about 45 percent of the tip of the beak in both phases. After breeding season, however, this bicoloring is not as obvious, and young reddish egrets have all dark bills. ● In high-breeding plumage, the colored phase exhibits an almost golden mane. The lores at this time are a turquoise blue. During breeding, the bill is strongly bicolored, and the bottoms of the feet and backs of legs are blue. When not breeding, the egret's lores, legs, and feet are blackish. ● During courtship, the male egrets become extremely aggressive and chase each other, stabbing at one another and locking bills in midflight. The head-toss display is often regarded as the bird's most important courtship ritual: Bristling and tossing back its neck and head feathers, the male secures his territory and walks back and forth in front of the female to win her approval. As the female moves closer, they may begin to rub their necks together. At this point they copulate, male on top, female on bottom.

The two different color phases of the reddish egret sometimes mate, producing mixed offspring, or the colored phase may mate with another colored phase and produce an occasional white offspring. Two paired whites always produce white offspring.

Since these birds are entirely coastal, they usually seek out islands where they nest in mixed colonies or alone. Many experts believe that waders prefer islands since there are fewer predators. This is especially true with reddish egrets, since they may build nests of twigs directly on the ground or in low shrubs and trees. Females lay three or four light bluish green eggs, each approximately 51mm in length. Both sexes incubate the eggs for twenty-six to twenty-seven days.

Because the nests are so low, raccoons and even Mexican coyotes can decimate entire nesting colonies. Bald eagles occasionally prey on adult reddish egrets, while grackles are the principal egg predator. Richard H. Pough, author of the *Audubon Water Bird Guide*, wisely cautions bird-watchers that "colonies should never be visited early in the breeding season, as these predators [such as grackles] can do tremendous damage if the herons are kept away from their nests."

Parents feed their young almost exclusively a diet of regurgitated fish bits, especially small fish such as the sheepshead minnow and the killifish. The young of the colored phase are gray with inch-long, rust-colored crown plumes. The white-phase young are solid white. The young typically leave the nest at four to five weeks, perching on nearby limbs or on the ground, while returning to the nest for feeding. Adults continue to feed their offspring until the young are about eight to ten weeks old, even though the young are able to fly at a little over six weeks. While nestlings are very vocal, adults are fairly silent. Adults in a colony may call more actively with a throaty *awwah,* but it is the bird's loud bill snap that attracts attention.

These birds' feeding habits are rather comical, as they like to run with their wings outstretched and their necks jerking from side to side. Then they halt abruptly to pursue schools of fish. This so-called "running feeding" or "canopy feeding" (with extended wings) helps the bird to first locate schools of fish and then shade the water before catching its prey.

Since reddish egrets are active feeders, they prefer open tidal flats six inches or less in depth. When feeding in water any deeper, they may hop, fly, or plunge to catch their prey. These birds are almost always found in marine habitats, where they usually feed alone but sometimes mix with other wading birds if their prey is abundant and concentrated. Young reddish egrets have been seen feeding together in small, shallow pools where minnows were plentiful. The birds are almost entirely diurnal, returning to roost in the evening.

Reddish egrets range from the Gulf of Mexico to the Caribbean and Bahamas. They are also found along Florida's eastern coastline and Gulf Coast north to Tampa Bay, as well as Mexico's Pacific Coast. There are an estimated four hundred nesting pairs in Florida, two-thirds of which are found in Florida Bay. The largest breeding numbers are along the Texas coast, where there are fifteen hundred nesting pairs — five hundred alone on Audubon's Green Island.

While some reddish egrets do fly south, they are not considered strong migrators.

Green Island
National Audubon Sanctuary

Green Island is part of the Laguna Madre Audubon Sanctuary, located on the southern coast of Texas. Approximately seven miles out in Laguna Madre Bay, this sandy island of some thirty acres is covered with densely twisted and thorny brush. Hackberry, torchwood, prickly pear, yucca, and the night-blooming cereus cactus provide cover to the world's largest reddish egret nesting area. Green Island is also the location of one of the largest nesting populations of roseate spoonbills.

The white ibis and white-faced ibis nest here, too, as well as eight species of herons and egrets.

As in most Audubon Society sanctuaries, visitors here must view the birds from a boat, and they are not allowed to set foot on the island. The sanctuary manager can arrange boat trips from time to time.

Nearby Boca Chica is recommended for viewing wading birds, since a boat is not necessary and visitors can walk along the open beaches. Wading birds can also be seen feeding in the open tidal flats all along the roadside and beaches.

Sanctuary Manager
Green Island National Audubon Sanctuary
P.O. Box 5052
Brownsville, TX 78532
(512) 541-8034

TOP: *Most birders love to observe the feeding habits of the reddish egret. The egret runs in zigzags, looking as though it might topple headfirst into the water.* ABOVE: *After feeding in J. N. "Ding" Darling National Wildlife Refuge, a reddish egret pauses to preen. After finishing its grooming, the bird resumes feeding.*

Range of the Reddish Egret

A cattle egret in full breeding plumage stands atop a palm frond on a Florida golf course. The golden back plumes and crest occur only during courtship. Cattle egrets exhibit different amounts of coloring; some birds turn almost completely golden.

Cattle Egret
BUBULCUS IBIS

One of the smaller white egrets, the cattle egret stands about twenty inches tall and has a twenty-seven-inch wingspan. Often seen feeding along interstate medians and pastures because it prefers to feed in short grass (rather than in shallow water), the cattle egret can be distinguished from the snowy egret by its yellow bill. The cattle egret is also a stockier-shaped bird, with short, dark green or green-yellow legs, pale yellow irides, and yellow lores. Even ornithologists have difficulty distinguishing the male from the female cattle egret except during the birds' copulation, when the female is on the bottom, or when she accepts twigs during nest building. ● During breeding, the white bird has patches of yellow-orange on its breast and back. The bird's crest is also yellow-orange during this time, as are its mantle and chest. (Once, in Venice, Florida, I saw a cattle egret colored completely yellow.) During high breeding, the cattle egret's legs, irides, and lores change color to a brilliant red. In some birds, the bill turns brilliant red with a yellowish tip, and the lores may appear to be violet. The crest is very prominent in both the male and female during this time; it is erected, along with the back feathers, to display for a mate. Snap displays (during which the egret moves its head up and down and snaps its beak), bill clapping, and stretch displays are all part of the pair bonding. The brilliant colors of both sexes begin to fade after the female has laid her eggs. ● This is one of the few egrets that may raise more than one brood during a season. This probably accounts for their large numbers, especially since they are relative newcomers to the North American continent, the first confirmed nesting being recorded in the United States in the 1950s in Florida and Texas. Cattle egrets originally migrated from Africa to South America, and later migrated to North America. ● Cattle egrets are highly colonial, nesting and roosting alongside other species of egrets and herons. Watching them fly in

LEFT: *Preening is a common activity of cattle egrets, which run their feathers through their beaks. The male stands near the nest, where he will roost for the night.* INSET: *Nesting quarters can become tight. A higher-nesting egret watches as a lower-nesting egret prepares to turn her eggs. Close nesting can cause frequent territorial disputes.*

great numbers to a roost is a truly amazing experience, as they may fly in groups of twenty to thirty at a time.

The nests are built in trees at heights ranging from just a few feet above the ground to more than forty feet. Both sexes build the nest and incubate four or five whitish eggs that are roughly 35 x 29mm in size; the female incubates at night while the male roosts nearby. The male defends his territory during nesting with great vigor and may become highly vociferous, emitting a coarse *raaa* sound.

The young, which hatch in three to three and one-half weeks, are covered with a light gray down, with a green base skin color. The young birds are fed in typical egret fashion through regurgitation; they soon become quite vocal with their *zitt, zitt* call, and at about three weeks of age the young begin to climb about surrounding tree limbs, abandoning the nest. The parents still feed them at this time, but in another three weeks the young are left to fend for themselves. These egrets are primarily terrestrial feeders, consuming insects such as grasshoppers, crickets, damsel- and dragonflies, and larvae, and small lizards, mice, and even small birds. Their favored technique for feeding is to follow any object or animal that will flush their prey, such as farm equipment, cattle (hence their name), or other large grazing animals. Cattle egrets prefer to feed in small groups. They may hop or fly after their prey, but usually they just walk fast. Cattle egrets look quite comical from a distance as they run frantically in pursuit of their prey, catching grasshoppers in mid-flight. The cattle egret's great success at extending its range to new continents is due to its preference for feeding in areas cleared by humans and planted with crops that attract insects which serve as an abundant food source.

Their range has extended dramatically in the fewer than forty years they have inhabited the North American continent. The cattle egrets' migrations carry them as far north as Canada, extending into Newfoundland along the Atlantic Coast. On the Pacific Coast, they range from Baja to British Columbia, and in the Midwest to North Dakota. They can be found along the entire coast of the Gulf of Mexico.

Yazoo National Wildlife Refuge Complex

The five refuges of the Yazoo National Wildlife Refuge Complex in west-central Mississippi contain 66,000 acres of hardwood forest, bald cypress, and tupelo sloughs, and shallow depressions containing button bush, water elm, swamp privet, and willow. All five refuges (Hillside, Panther Swamp, Yazoo, Mathews Brake, and Morgan Brake) contain many species of wading birds, including the cattle egret, great blue heron, great egret, snowy egret, little blue heron, and green-backed heron. In total, nearly 250 different species of birds inhabit the refuge during the year.

A few miles of trails exist in the different refuges, as well as paved and gravel roads, allowing access to the birds' habitat.

The principal office of the complex is located on Yazoo National Wildlife Refuge, about twenty-five miles south of Greenville, Mississippi. From state Highway 1, turn onto Yazoo Refuge Road, which winds through the forests and sloughs to the headquarters.

Refuge Manager
Yazoo National Wildlife Refuge Complex
Route 1, Box 286
Hollandale, MS 38748
(601) 839-2638

Range of the Cattle Egret

TOP: *Cattle egrets follow "beater" animals like horses, cows, and even tractors whose motions cause insects to reveal themselves. These little egrets appear in the middle of interstate medians, or on farm land, but are rarely seen feeding in water.* ABOVE: *The cattle egret's great success at furthering its range is due to its preference for feeding in areas planted with crops that attract insects such as grasshoppers, an abundant food source for the egret.*

Black-crowned Night-Heron
NYCTICORAX NYCTICORAX

One of the stockier herons, the black-crowned night-heron is less often seen due to its nocturnal habits. It stands approximately twenty-five inches, but with its neck pulled in, the bird appears shorter and heavier. Its broad wings sport a forty-six-inch wingspan. ● The bird derives its name from its black crown, and it also has black plumage on its back. The night-heron's wings are gray, with a light gray line that runs over the red irides and forehead. The sides of the black-crowned night-heron's head are white, and two or three long, thin white plumes extend from the back of the head. Its thick, dark bill curves down slightly, and its neck and legs are shorter than most other herons. The lores are blue with a slight tinge of green; legs and feet are yellow. During high breeding, the beginning of the courtship period when both sexes are preparing to mate, the long plumes reach a length of nearly one foot, and the lores and legs turn red. The male black-crowned night-heron is larger than the female and has a deeper voice. The birds are especially noisy when flying to and from the nest, calling their characteristically deep *quok* or *woc, woc, wock*. ● Juvenile black-crowned night-herons are easily confused with juvenile yellow-crowned night-herons. The young birds have orange eyes, yellowish green legs, and dark brown plumage with cream spots and streaks. Juveniles attain their slightly brownish adult plumage after approximately one year. ● Nesting takes place when the birds are two to three years old, and usually the birds group in a colony to nest. When nesting among other species, the heron prefers to nest under the canopy of trees, making it harder for predators such as crows to see through the vegetation. Anyone who ventures under a tree where a black-crowned heron has built a nest is in for

OPPOSITE INSET: *A short stout body and broad wings are prominent features of a black-crowned night-heron as it returns from the far shore with a nesting twig. Some heronries have a near-continuous flow of birds flying in and out gathering nesting material. During this time the herons are extremely vocal.* OPPOSITE: *Black-crowned night-herons are loud and protective when defending a nest site. Their nests are located closer to the interior of an island than those of most herons and egrets.*

quite an unpleasant surprise, as the bird excretes a large amount of a chalky white liquid, due to its unusual ability to digest all but the largest of bones from its prey. The stench on a nesting island at times can be unbearable.

Courtship among these night-herons can be very entertaining, with the males displaying for the female. First, the male bird bows and stretches, then rocks back and forth from foot to foot. He then hisses and claps his bill during the display. Allo-preening, when one bird rubs its bill over the head, neck, or back of its mate, regularly takes place after pairing. When greeting one another, the birds stretch their necks horizontally and erect the plumes on their heads while rubbing bills. Like the great blue heron, the male black-crowned grabs the female by the neck or head and stands on her back. He spreads his wings and flaps to keep balanced while the pair copulates.

I have seen several nests in the same cedar tree on an island in the middle of a Tennessee lake. The adult birds constantly flew back and forth all day long as they collected nesting twigs from the far shoreline. It was not uncommon for a half-dozen birds to be flying overhead at a time. The female black-crowned night-heron lays three to five pale blue eggs in her rather fragile nest; the eggs are approximately 53 x 37mm and are incubated by both parents for about twenty-one days. The young, which are covered with gray down, are fed by regurgitation (after a short while, the adults regurgitate directly into the nest). The young, which are quite noisy, begin to climb from the nest at about three weeks. White filaments stick up from their heads, their beaks are a dull yellow, and their feet are green. After six or seven weeks, the young birds fledge.

The black-crowned feeds during the night or early morning, although in Florida the night-heron may be fairly active even during the day. It is a fairly solitary feeder, usually standing or walking slowly in search of fish, crabs, amphibians, or mollusks; they also have been known to eat nestling egrets. The night-heron has a serrated beak, allowing it to hold onto slippery prey while shaking and beating it into a stupor. The bird then flips its meal headfirst, to be swallowed whole. In Flamingo, inside Florida's Ev-erglades National Park, black-crowned night-herons hang around the marina where artificial lights attract marine life within striking range. In Tennessee, the night-heron frequents dams where spotlights attract small minnows.

The black-crowned night-heron migrates in large flocks and breeds on every continent except Antarctica and Australia. It ranges across most of North America, except for the Southwest and a strip straight north. The black-crowned night-heron and the great blue heron are often the most common herons in most northern states.

Chincoteague National Wildlife Refuge

Located on the Virginia portion of Assateague Island, a barrier island, the Chincoteague National Wildlife Refuge encompasses more than thirteen thousand acres of beaches, salt marshes, and freshwater impoundments. Loblolly pines, oaks, myrtle, and bayberry cover the refuge, which is situated beneath the Atlantic Flyway.

Located in the channel between the refuge and mainland, small nesting colonies litter the waterscape. Glossy ibises, great egrets, tricolored herons, snowy egrets, little blue herons, great blue herons, cattle egrets, and yellow- and black-crowned night-herons can all be found feeding along the freshwater impoundments.

A three-and-one-half-mile loop drive begins at the refuge visitor center. Concessionaires run boat tours and a land tour that carries visitors down the seven-and-one-half-mile service road and back. Visitors may not drive on the service road, but walking is permitted.

From Pocomoke City, Maryland, drive south on Highway 13, and turn east on 175 to Chincoteague Island. Follow refuge signs to the visitor center.

Refuge Manager
Chincoteague National Wildlife Refuge
Box 62, Maddox Boulevard
Chincoteague, VA 23336
(804) 336-6122

OPPOSITE TOP LEFT: *Crabs are a favorite food for night-herons. The birds walk along the shore's edge until they spot their prey, which they seize with their beaks. When feeding their nestlings, night-herons may be seen during daylight hours, although the birds are predominantly nocturnal.* OPPOSITE BOTTOM: *Immature black-crowned and yellow-crowned night-herons are similar in their markings. These cryptic markings allow the birds to blend in well.*

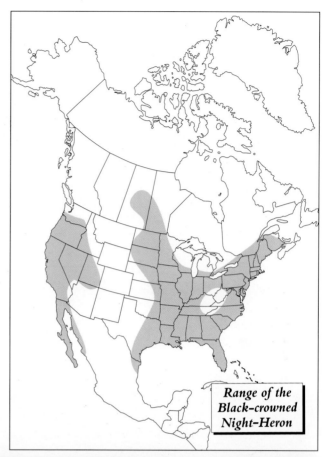

Range of the
Black-crowned
Night-Heron

Green-backed Heron
BUTORIDES STRIATUS

This is the smallest of North American herons, standing only sixteen to eighteen inches with a wingspan of twenty-six inches. The heron's crown, a dark bluish to greenish black, is raised when the bird is agitated by predators or other intruders. The color of its sharp bill is charcoal to black, and its irides are yellow. The heron's short legs range in color from greenish yellow to orange; its back plumage is a greenish gray; its throat is white with a chestnut-brown neck. The adult's breast is streaked with white and brown; juveniles are streaked and spotted, with yellowish legs and bill. The green-backed heron's neck is shorter than most herons', but it also looks shorter because of the bird's habit of keeping its head pulled back on its shoulders while resting and waiting for prey to approach within striking distance. ● The green-backed heron, whose common name is likely to change to simply "green heron," is quite vocal. Some of the bird's vocalizations have resulted in some interesting (and vulgar) nicknames, especially since one of its habits when agitated is to defecate while making a sharp *skeow* sound before flying off. ● During the green-backed heron's courtship, its breeding plumage does not change dramatically in length (unlike the great and snowy egrets' long back and tail aigrettes), although the occipital crest feathers do become a bit longer. The bird's lores tend to become a bluish black, and its bill turns a shiny black. The eyes and legs become a deep orange in both sexes. This bird's courtship is nothing short of comical, as the male hops from one foot to the other while the female sits in dense brush watching him erect his neck feathers and calling a soft *qua-qua*. ● Copulation takes place repeatedly; in between pairings, the male selects the nesting site and begins bringing twigs to the female. Nest construction is probably the poorest in the heron family: Ground-level observers might see the green-backed heron's eggs when looking up at the nest, which is usually built ten to thirty feet up in a tree. Cedars and maples are popular sites in the bird's range in Tennessee, especially those

A young green-backed heron exhibits the iridescent green feathers that earned it its name. This heron's orange bill and the down on its crown alert onlookers to the bird's age.

TOP: *A green-backed heron walks across a shallow pond covered with duckweed. It watches for dragonflies that land on the surface and for aquatic creatures that emerge through the vegetation.* ABOVE: *An agitated green-backed heron raises its crest and prepares to chase another green-backed that has entered its feeding territory. Green-backed herons blend in with their environment more easily than do larger herons.*

ABOVE: *This little heron casts a perfect reflection as it waits for unsuspecting prey to swim within striking distance.*

located near a stream, river, or pond. The birds are not as colonial as other herons, usually building no more than one nest per tree and maybe one to a half-dozen nests in a fifty-yard radius. When these herons nest in mixed colonies (that is, colonies of several different species such as great egrets, tricolored herons, and white ibises), the secretive green-backed heron is forced to build its nest in areas that larger herons, because of their size, cannot penetrate, usually under the canopy of foliage. This is one reason bird-watchers find green-backed herons' nests to be rarely visible.

The female lays four to five greenish blue eggs that are approximately 38 x 28mm and are incubated by both sexes. The incubation period is approximately three weeks, after which the chicks emerge covered with a grayish down. The young are good climbers, venturing out after one or two weeks and using their wings and beaks to help them climb. I once saw a green-backed heron not more than two weeks old standing out all alone in the early-morning sun and climbing from branch to branch in the swamp area of the St. Augustine Alligator Farm in Florida. The young chicks in the beginning are fed by the parent regurgitating food into the nest; the parent then picks up small pieces of food and inserts them into the waiting chicks' mouths. As the young grow older, the adult feeds them in typical heron fashion by regurgitating food directly into their beaks, although at this time the green-backed heron does not predigest the food delivered to the chicks, as other species do.

Its style of feeding and cryptic markings would make the green-backed heron a hard bird to see if it were not so widespread and common. Adult birds perform most of their feeding chores in the early morning and late evening. One of the more common feeding techniques involves crouching low on a floating log or reeds until a small fish or insect comes within striking range. The green-backed heron also perches on limbs overhanging the water's edge and moves slowly forward, closer and closer to the water's surface, until it can jab any small fish, insect, amphibian, or crustacean that happens by. (Once, while observing this latter fishing technique, I noticed an alligator that had also been watching the heron for some time. The alligator submerged itself completely, then thrust upward through the water and grabbed the bird. After pulling the heron underwater, the alligator surfaced and, with two or three snaps of its jaws, swallowed the bird. Only a few stray feathers were left floating near the marina, announcing a heron had once been there.) Another feeding technique used by the green-backed heron is to walk slowly through shallow water, stirring and raking with its feet to catch its prey.

One marvelous display of ingenuity was recorded at a zoo, where a wild green-backed heron liked to fish in a freshwater pool. The heron would fly over to the animal-food vending machines and pick up bait pellets that visitors had dropped on the ground. The bird then would drop the pellets into the water and wait for the minnows to swim up and nibble at the food. The heron would then proceed to catch its fill of minnows.

Its breeding range extends from Nova Scotia to the West Indies, Central America, and most of South America. Some are year-round residents of coastal California, southern Arizona, southern Texas, northern Florida, and South Carolina. Populations also winter in southern states, as well as in Mexico and Panama.

Upon witnessing the spring migration of the green-backed heron in 1840, John James Audubon wrote:

> I have observed their return in early spring, when arriving in flocks of from twenty to fifty individuals. They would plunge downwards from their elevated line of march, cutting various zig zags, until they would all simultaneously alight on the tops of the trees or bushes of some swampy place, or on the borders of miry ponds. These halts took place pretty regularly about an hour after sunrise. The day was occupied by them, as well as by some other species especially the blue, the yellow-crowned, and night-herons, all of which at this period traveled eastward, in resting, cleansing their bodies, and searching for food. When the sun approached the western horizon, they would at once ascend in the air, arrange their lines and commence their flight, which I have no doubt continued all night.

Arthur R. Marshall Loxahatchee National Wildlife Refuge

The mission of Loxahatchee National Wildlife Refuge is to maintain a suitable habitat for a wide variety of wildlife native to the northern Everglades. Wading birds, as well as American alligators, are abundant in the refuge, and can easily be spotted along the trails and canals.

During the year, Loxahatchee hosts nearly 250 different species of birds including the green-backed heron, black-crowned night heron, cattle egret, great blue heron, great egret, little blue heron, tricolored heron, and white

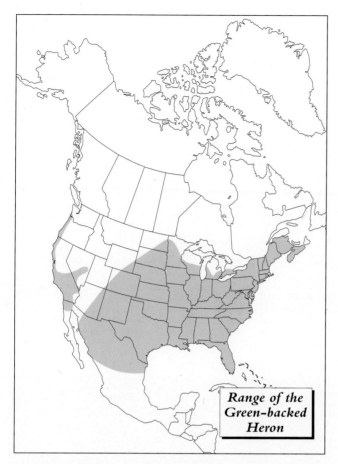

Range of the
Green-backed
Heron

ABOVE RIGHT: *A young green-backed, still partially covered with down, climbs out of its nest to watch for a parent returning with food. These small herons are excellent climbers, using their feet and beaks to help them move through thick foliage.*

ibis. The 145,635 acres of wet prairies, sloughs, sawgrass marshes, tree islands, and cypress swamps teem with these species, all of which nest in the refuge.

Loxahatchee encourages photography and wildlife observation, offering a cypress boardwalk, a marsh trail with an observation tower, and a 5.5-mile Everglades Canoe Trail. Almost half of the marshland in the refuge is open to public use, and with such an abundant wading bird population, the refuge should tickle pink your average wading bird watcher. In addition, Loxahatchee offers a visitor center with exhibits and information, early morning bird-watching walks, photography workshops and exhibits, and special interpretive programs given by area professionals.

Loxahatchee lies just southwest of West Palm Beach. The main entrance to the refuge is located off of U.S. Highway 441 between Boynton Beach Boulevard and Atlantic Avenue.

Refuge Manager, Arthur R. Marshall Loxahatchee
National Wildlife Refuge
Route 1, Box 278
Boynton Beach, FL 33437
(407) 734-8303

Yellow-crowned Night-Heron
NYCTICORAX VIOLACEUS

It is hard to mistake this medium-sized, stocky gray bird for any other heron. Standing at about twenty-six inches with a forty-two-inch wingspan, the yellow-crowned night-heron can be found throughout most coastal regions of North America, except along the Pacific, and up the lower Mississippi valley. It is also very common in the dank Atchafalaya Swamp in Louisiana. ● The yellow-crowned night-heron's head appears disproportionately large, with a medium-sized neck. The bird's black head sports a yellowish cream–colored crown and white cheek patches. Though primarily gray in color, the heron has darker back feathers with charcoal-colored centers and lighter margins. The irides are orange, and the lores are gray with tinges of yellow. The yellow-crowned night-heron's dusky yellow legs have black markings, and its bill is heavy and black. Both sexes look alike, with long occipital plumes. During breeding, the bird's bill turns a shiny black, the iris and legs a brilliant red, and the lores a dark green. ● The immature yellow-crowned night-heron can easily be confused with the immature black-crowned. Brown with cream-colored streaks and spots, the immature yellow-crowned takes almost three years to acquire its full adult plumage. ● More than twenty different calls have been attributed to this species, from flight calls to the greeting *wok* and *huk* calls between the bonded pair. Yellow-crowned night-herons exhibit the usual heron courtship behavior, including stretch displays, circle flights, bill clapping, and crest raising. Once, while visiting a wildlife refuge, I saw a male yellow-crowned night-heron fly in to present a twig to his mate. He then erected his back plumes to form a

A yellow-crowned night-heron watches for horseshoe crabs that swim close to shore. Most feeding is done at night by these solitary feeders. Its shorter, stouter neck indicates that it does not rely on stabbing its prey as much as the longer-necked egrets and herons.

LEFT: *An adult yellow-crowned night-heron and its young watch the other parent as it flies in to feed the young.* TOP: *Night-herons stand for hours in or under mangrove trees, resting during the daylight hours. These birds rarely stay this close to water for too long, since alligators would likely try to sneak up on them.* INSET ABOVE: *A male yellow-crowned night-heron collects nesting twigs to bring back to its mate. Nests are usually not as detectable as are those of other herons and egrets. As the male night-heron prepares to pass a nesting twig, it greets the female with crest raising and back-plume raising. The female constructs a substantial nest by heron standards.*

striking fan of feathers. His display reminded me of the way a peacock struts before a prospective mate. The male protects its nesting area with forward displays, in which it leans forward and thrusts its beak at any intruders. Courtship continues through nest building, when the birds can be seen rubbing their bills across one another's backs and raising their back plumes. As nest building continues, the male night-heron collects twigs for the female, which builds a sturdy nest and lays from three to five pale blue eggs. Both sexes incubate the eggs for a little over three weeks.

Night-herons typically nest in colonies and groups smaller than those of other herons. The nest usually is ten to thirty feet above the ground, and it usually is close to water. Although these birds can be quite loud when nesting, I have also seen them fly in and out of nesting colonies while uttering very few sounds. In particular, one city park in Florida that has approximately twenty nests has slides, swings, and sandboxes beneath the birds. Curiously, almost no one in the community was aware the night-herons were nesting there, even though the birds regularly flew in and out to feed their young.

Hatchlings are covered with gray down with thicker tufts on their crowns. Both parents feed the young, usually by regurgitating or dropping food directly into the nest (rarely into the bill in typical heron fashion). The young have dark yellow eyes and fledge at about twenty-five days.

Night-herons prefer standing along shorelines or walking slowly while searching for food. Much of their feeding, it seems, is related to the tide. At low tide, the night heron frequents the exposed tidal flats, wading and fishing the shallow waters. They feed much more often at night, as their name implies, but can also be seen feeding during the day, usually in the early morning or late evening. They catch fiddler crabs, horseshoe crabs, crayfish, fish, mussels, and other crustaceans. John James Audubon's *Journals* reveal much about the yellow-crowned night-heron:

> This species is by no means entirely nocturnal, for I have seen it searching for food among the roots of mangroves at all hours of the day, and that as assiduously as any diurnal bird, following the margins of rivers, and seizing on both aquatic and terrestrial animals. Whilst at Galveston, I frequently saw a large flock similarly occupied. When they had satisfied their hunger, they would quietly remove to some safe distance toward the middle of an island, where, standing in a crouching posture on the ground, they presented a very singular appearance. That they are able to see to a considerable distance on fine clear nights, I have no doubt, as I am confident that their migratory movements are usually performed at such times, having seen them, as well as several other species, come down from a considerable height in the air, after sunrise, for the purpose of resting and procuring food. When in numbers, and surprised on their perches, they usually rise almost perpendicularly for thirty or forty yards, and then take a particular direction, leading them to some well-known place. Whenever I have startled them from the nest, especially on the Florida Keys, they would sneak off on wing quite low, under cover of the mangroves, and fly in this manner until they had performed the circuit of the island, when they would alight close to me, as if to see whether I had taken their eggs or young.

The yellow-crowned night-heron's breeding habitat ranges from Florida to New York along the Atlantic Coast. The birds are found along the entire Gulf of Mexico, continuing up the Mississippi River and into the Ohio Valley. They also can be found in Nova Scotia and Newfoundland and may migrate as far south as Panama.

Tampa Bay Audubon Sanctuaries

Located six miles from downtown Tampa, Florida, is a group of ten islands, approximately three hundred acres in total, representing one of the nation's most important colonial nesting sites.

The two major spoil islands referred to as the Allafia Bank are covered with black, red, and white mangroves as well as cabbage palm, mulberry, and the exotic Brazilian pepper. During the 1993 nesting season, more than ten thousand pairs of birds nested on these two islands alone. While the featured nesting birds are the reddish egret and the roseate spoonbill, the other nesting wading birds include the great egret, little blue heron, green-backed heron, white ibis, glossy ibis, great blue heron, snowy egret, tricolored heron, cattle egret, and the black- and yellow-crowned night-herons. Three species of terns nest in the open areas.

Access to the sanctuary is highly restricted so that the

birds will not be disturbed. Inquiries should be addressed to the sanctuary manager. Areas open to the public for viewing these species are Lettuce Lake Park, which has a boardwalk through it; McKay Bay Park, located one mile from downtown Tampa; Honey Moon Island State Park in Clearwater; and Fort De Soto Park in St. Petersburg.

Sanctuary Manager
Tampa Bay Audubon Sanctuaries
410 Ware Boulevard, Suite 500
Tampa, FL 33619
(813) 623-6826

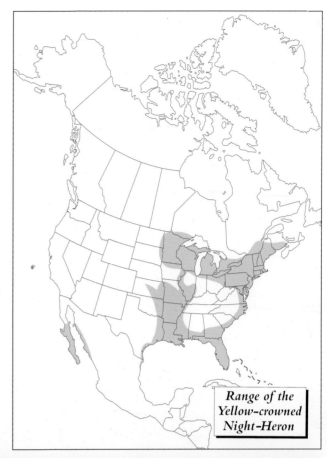

Range of the Yellow-crowned Night-Heron

BELOW: *Bill rubbing is part of the bonding and courtship ritual performed by yellow-crowned night-herons.*

White Ibis
EUDOCIMUS ALBUS

Of the three species of ibises that occur in North America (white, white-faced, and glossy), the white ibis is the most numerous. A solid white bird with black wing tips, this ibis stands approximately twenty-six inches with a forty-inch wingspan. The white ibis has no filamentous plumes; instead, its feathers are sleek. Its irides are pale blue, the bird's face is bare and reddish, and its legs and beak are both an orange-pink. The male white ibis is generally a bit larger than the female. Juveniles are dark brown, with a white belly and conspicuous white rump patch; they do not molt until they are one and one-half to two years of age. Juveniles' legs are bluish, and their irides are brown. ● White ibises make an almost nasal-like grunting noise. At Paurotis Pond in Everglades National Park, it is always evident when they are flying in to roost for the evening. The birds fly in only fifteen feet overhead, sending up a loud noise as the air streams through their wings. They fly with rapid wing beats and outstretched heads and necks in long lines usually fairly low to the ground, no more than 150 feet up. Still, on occasion they can be seen riding thermals in a spiral. ● These birds customarily probe with their slender bills along beaches as waves wash up around their long legs—waves that send shorter-legged shore birds scurrying up the sandy banks. White ibises also feed in fresh and brackish water, where they find crustaceans, crayfish, insect larvae, and cutworms. It is not unusual for a larger, more aggressive heron to attempt to steal freshly caught prey from an ibis. ● At the onset of the breeding season, the skin on the bird's face becomes bright red with a prominent red gular (throat) sac, which is thought to play a role in the courtship display. The bird's legs also become a brilliant crimson. Just prior to courtship, the birds' colors change, the male's more dramatically than the female's. At this time, the male makes clucking and cooing sounds and engages in bill snapping and stretching. The male and female rub bills together and even stroke one another with their bills. ● Approximately one-third of white ibises

Poor water management practices in the Everglades have caused the loss of many former feeding habitats of ibises. This white ibis feeds north of the Everglades near Fort Meyers.

nest in Florida, although there are other large colonies in places like the Audubon Society's Battery Island on the North Carolina coast and in the swamps of southern Louisiana. They will nest in mixed colonies, where they sometimes form dense groupings. Colonies in the Everglades, on coastal South Carolina, and in Louisiana may contain five thousand to twenty thousand nests. The nest placement ranges from ground level to almost twenty feet high. Poor water management practices in the Everglades have caused the loss of much of the former feeding habitat for the ibis, resulting in a sharp reduction in the number of birds that nest in this region.

I have also seen white ibises nest in dense groups on small islands on major golf courses in southern Florida, where the ibises seemed to be more numerous than the smaller egrets, such as snowies and cattle egrets.

The female white ibis lays three or four eggs, approximately 58 x 40mm, which are cream colored with brown blotches. Both sexes incubate for three weeks. At this time, the parent birds' chief enemies are fish crows, which rob the nests of eggs. When they hatch, the young have black heads and gray down; their beaks are flesh-colored with bands of black. In 1840, John James Audubon wrote:

> The young birds, which are at first covered with thick down of a dark gray color, are fed by regurgitation. They take about five weeks to be able to fly, although they leave the nest at the end of three weeks, and stand on the branches, or on the ground, waiting the arrival of their parents with food, which consists principally of small fiddler crabs and crayfish. On some occasions, I have found them at this age miles away from the breeding places, and in this state they are easily caught. As soon as the young are able to provide for themselves, the old birds leave them, and the different individuals are then seen searching for food apart.

Summer may find the white ibis relatively far north on the Atlantic Coast. The birds nest northward to North Carolina and southward to the coastal areas of South America and into northwest Peru. They are most numerous throughout Florida, along the Gulf of Mexico, and along the southern Atlantic coast.

Battery Island Audubon Sanctuary

Located just one-half mile offshore of Southport, North Carolina, is the state's largest wading bird nesting colony managed by the National Audubon Society. Battery Island comprises approximately one hundred acres of sandy beaches, salt marshes, and shrub thickets. The southern portion of the island is made up of dredge material. Here the silvering brush, red cedar, and yaupon support up to five thousand pairs of nesting white ibises, with egrets and herons mixed in. The northern section of the island, which has been left untouched, is covered with live oak, red cedar, and yaupon. Snowy egrets, tricolored herons, cattle egrets, little blue herons, great blue herons, glossy ibises, and black-crowned night-herons all nest here.

The heronry may be viewed offshore from a boat. No one is permitted to land on Battery Island without being accompanied by an Audubon staff person.

From the Southport waterfront, ibises, egrets, and herons can be seen as they fly in by the hundreds at sunset. This spectacle lasts for about one hour.

Sanctuary Manager
North Carolina Coastal Islands
P.O. Box 5223
Wrightsville Beach, NC 28480
(919) 256-3779

OPPOSITE TOP RIGHT: *The crimson legs and beak indicate the white ibis is in full breeding color.* OPPOSITE BOTTOM: *An island in the middle of a water hazard on a south Florida golf course hosts a colony of nesting white ibises. The juvenile white ibises have dark brown feathers.*

**Range
of the
White Ibis**

ABOVE: *Sunlight causes the feathers of the glossy ibis to reveal their bright iridescence. The glossy has a small white area on its face that leads many people to confuse the bird with the white-faced ibis.* OVERLEAF: *A silhouetted glossy ibis feeds in St. Mark's National Wildlife Refuge. Ibises usually feed in small groups.*

Glossy Ibis
PLAGADIS FALCINELLUS

You'd need a good pair of binoculars to distinguish the glossy ibis from the white-faced ibis, since both have light coloring around the face and dark iridescent plumage. From your vantage point, you would see that the irides are brown in the glossy ibis and reddish in the white-faced ibis. The birds' leg coloring is different too, for the glossy has long grayish black legs and feet, while the white-faced has dark reddish legs. ● The glossy ibis stands approximately twenty-two to twenty-three inches tall and has a three-foot wingspan. It is the smallest of the ibises and has the ibis's typically downward-curved beak. The adult plumage of the glossy is a deep chestnut color with an iridescent green and purple, especially noticeable when the sun is out. The juveniles are a dark grayish brown, with white streaking on the neck and a greenish iridescence. ● The glossy ibis seldom feeds alone, preferring small groups. In fact, it often moves in and out of mixed groups of herons. The ibis uses its long slender beak to probe for cutworms, crayfish, grasshoppers, fish, and mollusks. As it walks, it looks around every so often for signs of danger. ● At Merritt Island National Wildlife Refuge in Florida, these birds frequent the shallow canals along the roadside, especially those near the shuttle launch pads and the John F. Kennedy Space Center. H. W. Kale considers glossies to be freshwater feeders in Florida, while in other areas they are more commonly found in estuarine habitats. ● During courtship, the pair make crooning noises. Generally the female selects the nesting site. The glossy ibis is highly territorial, preferring to nest with its own species. In fact, it drives off any bird that attempts to nest within eight to twelve feet of its own nest, which is built from ten to twenty feet up in dense foliage. In 1913, naturalist Oscar E. Baynard made this observation about the glossy: "The disposition of the old glossy ibis toward the other ibis and herons is not good. I will have to admit that the glossy is pugnacious towards them, and one will never find an occupied nest of any other species as near as ten feet to a glossy nest

when they have reached the point where it is about time for the young to hatch. They will run off ibis and herons regardless of size, and all the other birds seem to recognize their superiority and leave. Then happens a peculiar thing. The fish crows will, of course, get the deserted eggs at once, and then the glossy ibis will begin dismantling these old nests, pulling them apart and dropping the sticks down on the ground, or in the water, whichever happens to be underneath, saving any sticks that appeal to them and taking them back to their own nest. I noticed that it took six days for this pair to dismantle 14 white ibis nests and 3 little blue heron nests that they had made leave. The worst of it was that one of the white ibis had baby young in, and when they died the glossies threw them out of the nest. It is barely possible, however, that the pair of white ibis that had used this nest were killed on their feeding grounds and failed to return, as this is the only instance where I ever noted the glossy dismantling a nest occupied by young.

Nesting colonies are fairly small. The mating pairs can be seen rubbing bills and preening one another much like wood storks. The female lays four greenish blue eggs, which are approximately 52 x 37mm. The eggs are incubated by both parents for twenty-one days. Hatchlings have a dark-colored down with a banded black and pinkish beak. Their feet are yellow, but they can do little but flop about. One parent stays with the hatchlings for roughly the first week, while the other collects food. The parent regurgitates food into its own throat, into which the young probe with their curved beaks.

After approximately two weeks, the young are climbing all about the branches of the nesting tree. Ibises are good climbers and swimmers, unlike many herons. When the young begin to fly, they travel with their parents sometimes up to twenty miles to feed before returning to the same evening roost.

The winter range of the glossy ibis does not extend much farther north than Merritt Island National Wildlife Refuge. It breeds from Maine to Florida along the Atlantic Coast and along the eastern Gulf Coast. Its breeding range extends into Central America and Venezuela.

Merritt Island National Wildlife Refuge

Located midway down Florida's Atlantic Coast is the 140,393-acre Merritt Island National Wildlife Refuge. This refuge consists chiefly of marshes that are brackish, both salt and fresh water, mixed with hammocks of palm, oak, and pine flatwoods. Numerous ponds and lagoons abound, the best known of which is named Mosquito Lagoon. Bird-watchers have recorded more than 280 different species of birds in the refuge, which is located beneath the Atlantic Flyway.

A strange dichotomy exists here between the primal marshes and the unmistakable signs of the Space Age, visible when one looks across the expanses of grasses and water toward a shuttle pad looming like an ancient monolith at the John F. Kennedy Space Center.

One of the best areas for observing birds is along the Black Point Wildlife Drive. Here, sandy roads have been built atop dikes that allow area managers to raise and lower the water from six to eighteen inches, creating ideal conditions for egrets, herons, and especially the glossy ibis. Since this area is not as heavily visited as refuges like J. N. "Ding" Darling National Wildlife Refuge, the birds are less tolerant of tourists. I find that a car is the best blind from which to watch the birds.

Merritt Island National Wildlife Refuge has a visitor center with interpretive exhibits and a small bookstore.

To reach the refuge, exit off I-95 onto East 406 near Titusville. This highway takes you to Black Point Wildlife Drive. To reach the refuge headquarters, take East 402, which branches off 406.

Merritt Island National Wildlife Refuge
P.O. Box 6504
Titusville, FL 32780
(407) 861-0667

OPPOSITE TOP LEFT: *Glossy ibises probe the shallow waters of a roadside ditch with a mixed group of egrets just across from the John F. Kennedy Space Center complex.* OPPOSITE BOTTOM: *Located beneath the Atlantic Flyway, Merritt Island National Wildlife Refuge has been home to more than 280 different species of birds.*

Range
of the
Glossy Ibis

White-faced Ibis

PLEGADIS CHIHI

Upon first glance, the white-faced ibis looks no different from the glossy ibis, which is probably why at one time it was called the white-faced glossy ibis. It stands approximately two feet tall with a thirty-nine-inch wingspan. It has the ibis's typically long, slender, downward-curved beak with white feathers around the edges of its bare face (the only real difference between the white-faced and the glossy). The white-faced ibis's irides are red, and its legs and feet are a dull, dusky red. ● From a distance, the bird appears black, but upon closer examination its feathers are deep purple, violet, and reddish bronze. The irides are evident when viewing the bird in direct sunlight. The white face becomes much more prominent during the courtship period, although there are no real changes in plumage patterns as there are in herons. The juvenile's plumage is first streaked with off-white and brown. The bird first acquires adult plumage on its head and neck, which later turns an iridescent greenish bronze. ● The white-faced ibis prefers marshes and lake margins, where it often roosts on mud banks. I have spent many hours watching these ibises probe into the muck in search of earthworms, snails, insects, small fish, and crayfish. They tend to glance up every thirty to sixty seconds to check for would-be predators. At Sabine National Wildlife Refuge in Louisiana, they feed alongside black-necked stilts, which act as sentinels by alerting the ibises to impending danger. White-faced ibises also are found feeding in large flocks with gulls in South American pastures. ● During courtship, the male and female rub bills and preen one another while making a cooing sound. They build the nest together, often in large nesting areas, using small twigs. The nests I have seen were built on top of spartina grasses, approximately twelve to eighteen inches off the ground, on Rabbit Island at the edge of Sabine National Wildlife Refuge. When I approached the island by boat, it looked deserted though covered with tall grasses. But as I drifted nearer to the shore, suddenly snowy egrets, tricolored

The bright red eyes and large rim of white identify this bird as a white-faced ibis.

herons, and white ibises all began rising from their nests and flying off. The white-faced ibises were always the last to reveal themselves and leave their nests.

The largest nesting population of white-faced ibises occurs along the Louisiana and Texas coasts, but they also nest as far north as Colorado and Oregon. The female lays three or four pale blue eggs, approximately 52 x 36mm, and both parents incubate the eggs — usually for about three weeks. After hatching, the young are covered with a blackish down. Their crowns are almost bare, with only a few white feathers, but these soon give way to a solid black down. The beak is a definite flesh color, with a black band around the middle and the tip.

When the young are old enough to move about, they may leave the nest if approached—since the nest is so close to the ground—to hide in the tall grasses, returning only when the intruder has departed.

In autumn, the birds in Oregon and Colorado migrate south to the Texas and Louisiana coasts. Some birds also migrate to the tropics.

The white-faced ibis flies with its neck outstretched and its feet extended behind its tail. The bird's wings beat rapidly. When migrating, the birds form long diagonal lines. Flock circle flights are not limited to the breeding season. In 1908, Dr. Frank Chapman wrote an interesting account about flocks of white-faced ibises circling overhead:

> In close formation, they soared skyward in a broad spiral, mounting higher and higher until, in this leisurely and graceful manner, they had reached an elevation of at least 500 feet. Then, without a moment's pause and with thrilling speed, they dived earthward. Sometimes they went together as one bird, at others each bird steered its own course, when the air seemed full of plunging, darting, crazy ibises. When about fifty feet from the ground, their reckless dash was checked and, on bowed wings, they turned abruptly and shot upward. Shortly after, like a rush of a gust of wind, we heard the humming sound caused by the swift passage through the air of their stiffened pinions.

White-faced ibises were hunted as game birds until the second decade of this century, although their numbers were not decimated like those of the herons, which were hunted for their plumes.

Malheur National Wildlife Refuge

Southeastern Oregon boasts one of the largest freshwater marshes (sixty-five thousand acres) west of the Mississippi River. Located in the northern Great Basin, this 186,000-acre area includes shallow marsh, sagebrush, and high desert. With only eight inches of rain annually, Malheur National Wildlife Refuge depends on snowmelt from the Steens Mountains.

Large areas of grass and marshes may hide the 230 nesting pairs of greater sandhill cranes (an additional eighty pairs nested adjacent to the refuge in 1993). Also nesting inside the refuge are seven thousand pairs of white-faced ibises. Other nesting wading birds include snowy egrets, great egrets, black-crowned night-herons, and great blue herons.

The center patrol road runs through the middle of the refuge for forty miles. Side roads total another fifteen miles, and there are three miles of walking trails.

In the fall, some three thousand greater sandhill cranes gather here for migration—usually about the first and second week of October. In the spring, during the first and second week of April, approximately fifteen thousand lesser sandhills migrate through.

Refuge headquarters is located in Frenchglen. From Burns, Oregon, take Route 78 east and turn right (south) on 205. Drive approximately twenty-five miles, then turn left at the refuge sign and travel another five miles to the refuge headquarters.

Refuge Manager
Malheur National Wildlife Refuge
HC 72, Box 245
Princeton, OR 97721
(503) 493-2612

OPPOSITE TOP: *A white-faced ibis parent stands up from its nest hidden in tall grass. These birds are usually the last in a mixed nesting area to leave the nest when approached.* OPPOSITE MIDDLE LEFT: *Three newly hatched white-faced ibises and an unhatched egg fill a ground-level nest on Rabbit Island near Sabine National Wildlife Refuge on the Louisiana coast.* OPPOSITE BOTTOM LEFT: *When approached, older chicks will climb out of the nest and hide in surrounding grasses. Once the intruder leaves, the young ibises return to their nest.*

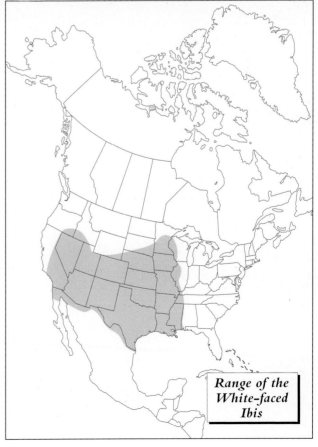

Range of the White-faced Ibis

Roseate Spoonbill
AJAIA AJAJA

It would be hard to mistake this bird for any other. The roseate spoonbill, which stands approximately thirty-two inches tall with a fifty-three-inch wingspan, has delicate pink body and wing feathers, and its shoulder coverts are a brilliant red. The bird's neck is white, and its tail feathers are an orange-pink. The spoonbill's bare head is green with a black stripe, making the bird resemble a bald man with a dark fringe of hair. The spoonbill's eyes are red, and as if this feature weren't enough to make the bird stand out, its long greenish gray bill is shaped like a spatula at the end—hence the name spoonbill. ● Unfortunately, the roseate spoonbill was prized by plume hunters at the turn of the century, when its pink wings were quite the fashion as fans. As a result, the spoonbill population was nearly decimated. Excluding sites in Mexico, where large numbers nest, today the only real breeding populations in North America occur in Florida and along the Gulf Coast into Louisiana and Texas. Nesting populations in Florida have recovered from a low of about fifteen pairs in the 1930s to over one thousand pairs at the present. ● Both the male and female spoonbill perform a courtship dance. The male, with its beautiful pink wings opened, draws closer and closer to the female with a series of short hops. After watching the male for a while, the female may reinforce his behavior by hopping in his direction. At this point, the pair begins a series of head-raising and lowering motions and bill clapping, followed by copulation at the nest site or nearby. Most spoonbills do not breed until their third year. ● Spoonbills prefer to nest in colonies in red and black mangroves, which may account for the larger breeding colonies near the Florida Keys. They nest earlier in Florida, usually beginning in November and finishing by March in Florida Bay, while the southwest Louisiana and Texas colonies nest from April to August. In Louisiana's Sabine National Wildlife Refuge, the spoonbills ground-nest on nearby islands in the middle of hundreds of laughing gulls, terns, tricolored and great blue herons, and

Three roseate spoonbill chicks huddle low to avoid detection in their nest constructed among tall grasses. If approached just a week later, these young would clamber from their nest and hide in the surrounding thickets.

ABOVE INSET: *When a low tide creates shallows in the early morning, large numbers of spoonbills and other waders gather to feed during the one- to two-hour event.* RIGHT: *An adult spoonbill exhibits its bare head and distinct red shoulder coverts. Most roseates prefer feeding early in the day; this one was photographed at Mrazek Pond in Everglades National Park.*

white-faced ibises.

Like most wading birds, the male presents the female with twigs while she constructs the nest; there may be bill clapping and ritualized greetings at twig presentation. The female lays three or four cream-colored eggs splotched with brown, approximately 65 x 44mm. Both birds incubate, and the eggs hatch in approximately twenty-four days.

Anyone who glimpses a young spoonbill will never forget its strange, disproportionate shape. Its body looks like a pink butterball turkey straight from the butcher, covered with a fine white down. The head and bill of a young spoonbill look more like those of a duckling than those of their parents, and the feet, legs, and bill are orangish.

The young birds flop feebly from side to side when trying to move about. The adult regurgitates partially digested fish and shrimp into its own beak for the young, which vigorously poke out bits to swallow whole. The disproportionate body size is obvious if a chick has hatched out five days before its younger sibling. Larger birds sometimes evict smaller ones when food is scarce. Adults often fly five to twenty miles from the colony to forage for food.

Ground-nesting can lead to the decimation of entire colonies if predators such as raccoons are able to locate them. Of course, these ground-nesting areas are always on islands away from the mainland, but predators might swim or get caught in a storm and wash up on the island. This also explains why whole colonies move from time to time. When young in the ground-nesting colonies are able to move about if approached, they will leave the nest and hide in tall grasses, returning after the intruder is gone.

At the age of approximately one month, the young, which now sport some feathers, begin to exercise their wings, climbing out onto surrounding foliage. After they have reached adult size, the young still can be recognized by the white feathers covering their heads and by their generally paler pink bodies and wings.

Spoonbills can be found feeding in shallow coastal bay areas, as well as in brackish and fresh water. Feeding is performed by partially submerging the spatulate bill, although I have also seen these birds stick their heads almost entirely underwater and sweep their bills in an arc from side to side while walking. The roseate spoonbill does not feed by sight; rather, like the wood stork, it catches its prey by feel, snapping its beak closed when the prey comes into contact with the bird. Then, pulling its beak out of the water, the bird swallows its quarry. Spoonbills feed more often in the early hours of morning or in late evening, but they will also feed at night. They sometimes emit a grunting noise during feeding.

After the young are old enough to be on their own, they scatter northward to feed. The J. N. "Ding" Darling National Wildlife Refuge on Sanibel Island in Florida is inundated with young birds during the months of May and June. Every morning from sunrise until 8:30 or 9:00 A.M., the birds feed in the shallow areas, especially when low tide coincides with sunrise.

Sabine National Wildlife Refuge

Located on the coast in the southwest corner of Louisiana, Sabine National Wildlife Refuge is the largest coastal marsh refuge on the Gulf of Mexico. Encompassing 139,308 acres, the habitat ranges from fresh water and brackish marsh all the way to ocean salinity.

The refuge headquarters is located on Route 27, where exhibits and personnel interpret the area. A loop trail one and one-half miles long winds through a marsh, where white-faced ibises, least bitterns, and snowy egrets can be seen searching for prey. An observation tower is located roughly halfway around the loop.

Sabine was established primarily to provide food and habitat for migrating winter waterfowl such as snow geese, which often number in the thousands. A boat is required to really see the wading-bird spectacle that occurs on Rabbit Island, about ten minutes from refuge headquarters. This island is home to ground-nesting roseate spoonbills, white-faced ibises, tricolored herons, great blue herons, great egrets, white ibises, snowy egrets, laughing gulls, and terns. Watch the birds from the comfort of your boat, since going ashore at almost any point on the island will disturb the birds by flushing them from their nests.

To reach Sabine, take I-10 to Sulphur, Louisiana, and travel approximately twenty miles south on Route 27.

Sabine National Wildlife Refuge
Highway 27, South 3000 Main Street
Hackberry, LA 70645
(318) 762-3816

Range of the Roseate Spoonbill

ABOVE: *A pink feather and three cream-colored, brown-blotched eggs alert biologists that this nest of reeds was woven by a spoonbill.* RIGHT: *In Sabine National Wildlife Refuge, Louisiana, roseate spoonbills ground-nest on nearby islands in the middle of hundreds of laughing gulls, terns, tricolored and great blue herons, and white-faced ibises.*

Wood Stork
MYCTERIA AMERICANA

Standing over three and one-half feet tall, this bird is the only stork native to North America (excluding Mexico). Formerly known as the wood ibis, it has been nicknamed "flinthead" by locals because of its gray, featherless head. "By any name," writes naturalist Archie Carr, "this bird epitomizes primeval Florida. . . . As far as I'm concerned, ironheads are esthetically indispensable." Its wingspan is more than sixty-five inches long, and the male weighs in at approximately ten pounds—a good three pounds heavier than the female. The wood stork's stout body is covered with white feathers, while its primaries and primary coverts are an iridescent greenish, bluish black. Without the aid of binoculars, many people mistake this large bird for a white pelican, especially when they see the bird soaring. A closer look at the bird in flight, however, reveals the distinctive long black legs, pinkish feet trailing behind the bird, and a fully extended neck. Its head and neck are bare, the skin a grayish black color. A horny plate is visible on the front of the head, and the irides are a dark brown. Its dusky gray bill is heavy and long, tapering to a downward curve. Like the spoonbill, it would be considered an ugly bird were it not for its beautiful plumage. ● This endangered species is considered the true barometer of South Florida's wetlands. The wood stork's migration pattern and its breeding cycle are both directly linked to the flooding and drying of southern swamps and marshes. The Corkscrew Swamp Sanctuary southeast of Fort Myers, Florida, has traditionally been the wood stork's single most important nesting habitat. Some years, due to insufficient rains and the resulting scarcity of fish, there may be no nesting. On the other hand, when there is too much rain, the water level may rise so high that fish are no longer trapped in smaller areas, scattering them over a larger area. Even the dumping of water from artificial canals into the lakes and swamps can negatively impact the wood stork. ● The ideal cycle consists of normal rains through the rainy season, June to October, providing an abundance

Wood storks, or "ironheads," excrete on their own legs, which helps the birds stay cooler when confined to the nest.

LEFT: *Wood storks have been known to fly more than one hundred miles each day to catch fish for their young.* TOP INSET: *The male wood stork stays busy collecting twigs and leaves for the construction and lining of the nest. He presents these to the female, which actually builds the nest.* ABOVE INSET: *The wood stork walks slowly when probing for small fish such as mollies and sailfin. When the stork's bill comes into contact with its prey, the bird's reaction time is said to be one of the fastest in the bird world.*

of fish and an ample water supply. During the dry season, when the water areas begin to shrink, fish are concentrated into smaller areas where the stork feeds. To catch its prey, the wood stork wades with its large beak submerged and partially opened; when the bill sweeps by something, it snaps shut. This remarkable snapping reflex is considered one of the fastest in the animal kingdom.

In Corkscrew Swamp, storks nest in cypress trees as tall as seventy or eighty feet. Sometimes more than a dozen pairs of wood storks will build their nests in the same tree and line them with Spanish moss or sprigs of green leaves. Some of the nesting twigs brought in by the male — especially those nesting on mangrove islands near Venice, Florida — still have foliage, which is then incorporated into the nest. Much bill clapping and neck rubbing take place during courtship as the pair prepares to copulate.

Corkscrew Sanctuary produces large numbers of sailfin mollies, crayfish, bluegills, and red-ear sunfish. The swamp eventually becomes fished out by the birds as the female wood stork builds the nest — a flimsy structure made from twigs supplied by the male, and as the pair begin to raise their offspring. The female typically lays three chalky white eggs, measuring approximately 68 x 46mm. Incubation, which takes around thirty days, is performed by both sexes, though primarily by the female.

When the young first hatch, they are covered with white down except for the front half of the head. Since the adults are still feeding in the nearby swamps — usually within five to twenty miles — they bring food, regurgitating it into the nest. The nestlings then grab the fish from the bottom of the nest.

As the young grow older, they are covered with brownish down and become considerably noisier — unlike their fairly quiet parents. The closer marshes become dry in winter and spring, and the parents, freed from having to shade the nestlings, are able to fly greater distances. So at this stage, the parents fly to feed around Fakahatchee Strand State Preserve and Big Cypress National Preserve to the south and southwest of Corkscrew. Near Big Cypress, they can be seen feeding along Highway 29 in water-filled ditches and along the Tamiami Trail. Should these areas become fished out, the adults have been known to fly over one hundred miles every day to feed in the marshes around Lake Okeechobee to the northeast. Storks feed approximately fifty pounds of fish to each nestling by the time the young are sixty days old and ready to fly. Most storks disperse northward to North Florida, Georgia, South Carolina, and Alabama during the rainy season (summer and fall) in South Florida.

During the 1960–61 breeding season, the Corkscrew Swamp rookery boasted some six thousand active nests. In 1992–93 however, heavy rains prevented nesting at the National Audubon Society–operated swamp, although more than one hundred nests were recorded in the Venice nesting rookery to the northwest along the coast. If rains raise water levels too high in the nesting grounds, the parents may abandon their young.

Wood storks soar in large numbers to great heights, riding thermals and spiraling out of sight. They conserve their energy by gliding a lot as they travel to feed. These birds look surprisingly comical when coming in for a landing, their large cupped wings flapping madly to slow themselves so as not to break their long, thin dangling legs.

Their breeding range is confined mostly to Florida, although as conditions for nesting have deteriorated, more and more pairs have nested in coastal areas of Georgia and South Carolina. In 1993, close to one thousand pairs nested in each of these two states. While they may range a bit northward, they are more dominant in the South along the coast of Mexico into Central and South America and Peru.

Corkscrew Swamp Sanctuary

Corkscrew Swamp Sanctuary, owned and operated by the National Audubon Society, fits most people's preconception of what the Everglades should look like.

Located near Immokalee, Florida (and little else), these eleven thousand acres contain the largest remaining stand of virgin bald cypress in the United States. Some of the largest trees are as old as six hundred years, and at the right time their tops are filled with the largest nesting colony of wood storks in existence.

Depending upon the year, the stork's nesting occurs between December and May, though the water level, which fluctuates as much as two feet depending on the rainfall, affects nesting more than the season. At nesting time, a portion of the mile-long boardwalks may be sectioned off to prevent disturbing the birds. Because of the loss of feeding habitats outside the sanctuary, storks no longer nest every year.

Several "lettuce lakes" are found here, where water lettuce blankets the surface of the water. (Due to extreme droughts, however, lettuce may not always be in abundance.) The floating vegetation appears quite stable, even when little blue herons walk across leaves to feed on insects and crustaceans around the plants.

Adjacent to the parking lot is a building where you pay admission and where guidebooks and other nature items can be purchased.

Near Naples, Florida, take I-75 to exit 17 near Naples Park. County Road 846 will lead to Sanctuary Road. There are sanctuary signs marking the way.

Corkscrew Swamp Sanctuary
Box 1875, RD 6 Sanctuary Road
Naples, FL 33940
(813) 657-3771

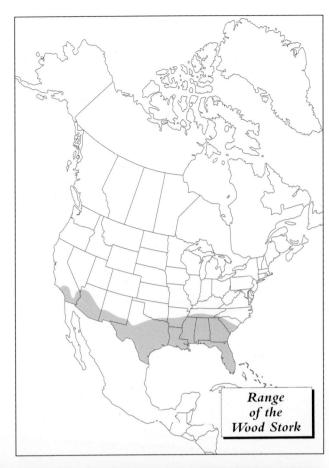

Range
of the
Wood Stork

BELOW: *When most people think of wood stork nesting areas, large cypress trees usually come to mind—but coastal mangrove islands, like this one near Venice, Florida, also host small nesting groups.*

Limpkin
ARAMUS GUARAUNA

Of all the long-legged water birds, the limpkin is likely the most closely associated with swamps in the South. This large-bodied brown bird stands approximately twenty-seven inches tall with a three-and-one-half-foot wingspan. Its legs range in color from charcoal to dark gray, with a tinge of green, and the bird uses its long toes to balance on floating vegetation like water lettuce. The limpkin's neck is slender, though not as long as the necks of many herons. Its plumage is short and brown with streaks of cream. The bird has brown irides and a long, slightly curved grayish brown beak. The juvenile has the same coloring but is paler. ● Limpkins generally fly fairly low and they seem to put forth a great deal of effort, much like an anhinga. When walking, the bird may flick its tail while moving its head in a jerking fashion, providing a hint of its relationship to rails and coots. The limpkin will emit a soft clucking sound and look almost agitated to onlookers. It also makes a loud and very distinctive call, *kur-r-ee-ow, kur-r-ee-ow, kurr-ee-ow, kr-ow, kr-ow,* which can be heard for great distances and often provides the only indication that limpkins are present. ● When searching for food, the limpkin wades slowly, probing for snails, frogs, worms, mussels, and insects. This bird prefers to feed in the early morning and late evening, and its favorite food is the pomacea, or apple snail, which it grabs and carries to a favorite feeding spot. After breaking through the snail's operculum, it extracts the snail and swallows it whole. The shell is then discarded along with other empty shells. This habit makes it easy to locate limpkins—just find their mounds of cast off shells. I once saw a limpkin grab a medium-sized turtle in Florida's Wakulla Springs State Park near Tallahassee, but I don't know what happened to the turtle, since the boat I was in was moving along rather briskly. ● Limpkins always hide their nests well, whether in masses of sawgrass or in cypress trees, often placing Spanish moss over the top to serve as a canopy. The female lays between five and eight cream-colored eggs, approximately

A limpkin aware of the photographer's presence watches alertly while making a clucking noise. After becoming accustomed to the photographer, this bird eventually resumed its search for food.

60 x 46mm. Unless you happen to be present on the day the eggs hatch, you won't be able to observe the babies in the nest, since the young leave within twenty-four hours. Hatchlings are covered with a rust-colored down, and they can swim as well as their parents.

Limpkins prefer freshwater marshes, swamps, creeks, and river banks. They seem to follow regular paths, almost like deer, and to haunt favorite feeding areas. Some birds may stand alone in cypress trees, while others stand in groups along shallow marshes. Limpkins prefer roosting in thick grasses, and they will move quietly away if agitated.

Limpkins range throughout all of Florida and into southeast Georgia. They are also found in Cuba, the West Indian Islands, and in freshwater wetlands from Mexico to Argentina.

Edward Ball Wakulla Springs State Park

Florida's Wakulla Springs State Park entertains nearly 175 species of birds in its 2,864 acres of hardwood forest, old-growth floodplain forest, and bald cypress trees. Like the tourists, wading birds flock to the park, where at different times of the year the observant birdwatcher can see limpkins, great blue herons, great herons, tricolored herons, little blue herons, snowy egrets, cattle egrets, green-backed herons, white ibises, and even the occasional wood stork. The birds feed and nest in the shallow marshes along the river.

The park offers tours on the river on boats that wind through the bald cypress islands. An observation platform overlooks the water, one of the world's largest and deepest freshwater springs. Glass-bottomed boat tours allow a clear view of the mouth of the spring cavern one hundred feet below. In addition, hiking trails snake through the forests, and regular interpretive tours and workshops help guests learn more about the birdlife of Wakulla Springs.

Edward Ball Wakulla Springs State Park sits about fifteen miles south of Tallahassee, Florida, at the intersection of state roads 61 and 267.

Edward Ball Wakulla Springs State Park
One Spring Drive
Wakulla Springs, FL 32305
(904) 922-3633

PREVIOUS PAGES: *An apple snail is visible here beneath the floating water lettuce. A limpkin will carry a snail to its favorite feeding spot, extract the snail and toss the shell into a pile of other discarded shells. Finding a pile of pomacea shells is an excellent way to locate limpkins.* PREVIOUS PAGES, INSET: *After feeding, a limpkin stretches and begins to preen. If disturbed, the bird will flick its tail nervously and walk about slowly before heading into dense grass. If really agitated, the bird will fly a short distance away from the intruder.* OPPOSITE TOP LEFT: *Limpkins find cypress and palm trees draped in Spanish moss and covered with bromeliads to be prime nesting trees. This limpkin watches as a boat passes beneath its nesting tree.* OPPOSITE BOTTOM: *Limpkins prefer freshwater areas for feeding, since apple snails—a major food source—are abundant in these areas. These snails lay hundreds of eggs on the stems of aquatic plants.*

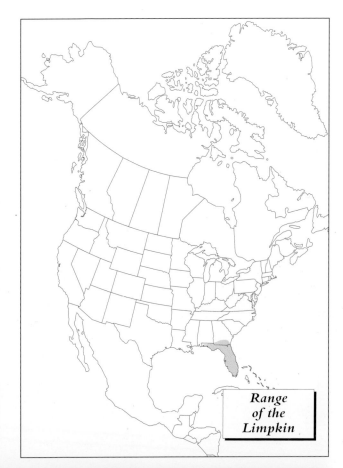

Range of the Limpkin

ABOVE: *The bare red flesh on the sandhill crane's forehead is this bird's distinctive mark for identification. The more excited the bird becomes, the redder its patch.* LEFT INSET: *Two young Florida sandhill cranes follow their parent into a shallow marsh to look for food. The young still have colors that allow them to blend in to their surroundings for protection against predators.*

Sandhill Crane
GRUS CANADENSIS

It is hard to mistake this tall gray bird for any other wader. There are six races of the sandhill: three migratory and three nonmigratory. The migratory birds are the greater, lesser, and Canadian; the nonmigratory races are the Florida, Cuban, and Mississippi sandhill cranes. The lesser sandhill, the smallest of the six, stands four feet tall with a six-foot wingspan. The lesser weighs in at about six pounds, while the greater sandhill weighs approximately ten pounds. All sandhill cranes' long necks are a lighter gray, as are their cheeks, which are almost white. The sandhill's bare crown is bright red, varying in intensity according to the bird's disposition (brighter when the bird is excited). Sandhill cranes have large and very sharp black beaks and long black legs, and the birds' irides range from brownish to bright orange. ● Sandhill cranes mate for life, and after pairing they perform elaborate dances and a unison call. Ornithologists think that a sandhill recognizes its partner's calls, allowing the birds to find one another when migrating, feeding, and roosting. The unison call is not used until the birds reach maturity at two to three years. The female calls twice to the male's single call, as he points his beak skyward and walks stiff-legged with his primaries lowered. As the male parades, both sexes' crowns become a brilliant red. The female sandhill readies for copulation by spreading her wings and lowering her body and neck (similar to the great blue heron). The male stands on her back, flapping his wings, until mating has occurred, after which the pair begin to preen vigorously. ● Sandhills generally return to the same nesting sites year after year, although the male may have to fend off other birds in the pair's territory. Because older wading birds, including the sandhill, are more experienced at finding food and surviving altogether, third-year adults do not seem to be as successful at nesting as fourth- and fifth-year birds are. ● The female sandhill builds the nest, which she'll usually place in shallow water. She begins by pulling vegetation into a mound above the water line; as she later sits on the nest,

OPPOSITE BOTTOM INSET AND ABOVE: *Sandhill cranes find refuge at their wintering grounds in New Mexico. Just before taking flight, sandhills become very alert. The cranes look about before taking a running leap and flapping their large wings. Then, when taking off, the birds make a loud trumpeting sound.* OPPOSITE TOP INSET: *In early morning, flocks of sandhills fly to nearby pastures to feed. The birds disperse across the field into looser groupings while probing for food.*

she continues to pull in nesting material. During this period, the birds rub rotting vegetation across their feathers, staining them to blend in with the nesting area. Should an intruder wander too near the nest, the birds will become quite vocal and aggressive—or even feign a broken wing to lure the predator away.

The sandhill lays two pale green eggs, approximately 97 x 63mm in size. Both sexes share incubation, which takes thirty days, with the female staying on the nest at night while the male roosts nearby. The female incubates when the first egg is laid; the male waits until both eggs are in the nest. During nesting, the adults molt, much like geese, which renders them flightless while raising their chicks.

The first chick, covered in a rusty brass-colored down, leaves the nest within twenty-four hours, accompanied by the nonincubating adult. About forty-eight hours after the first chick hatches, the second breaks out from its egg; it leaves the nest accompanied by the other adult shortly thereafter. The young are usually fed insects, but they also eat seeds and roots—and sometimes even the eggs and young of other marsh-nesting birds. Young sandhills hatched on the Arctic tundra have a different diet, feeding primarily on lemmings. It will take some two months for the young to learn to fly, which is why most parents and their young feed in tall grasses well hidden from predators.

The three races of migratory cranes follow a number of flyways. The best known stopover is the Platte River near Kearney, Nebraska, where lesser sandhill cranes numbering as many as 400,000 may roost on the Audubon Society's Lillian Annette Rowe Sanctuary. The lesser makes up about 90 percent of the three races on the Platte. Bosque del Apache National Wildlife Refuge in New Mexico has predominantly greater sandhill cranes. Although migratory cranes can fly over three hundred miles in one day, they usually cover only about two hundred miles.

Weather can almost be predicted by the bird's migratory behavior. If bad weather is approaching, the birds land early. Their normal roosting time is sunset; by one hour after sunrise, they are well on their way again, usually flying off in small groups.

The sandhill's posture signals when the bird is ready to take flight: First, it stretches its neck out horizontally, then it runs into the wind, jumping up as it flaps its large wings, rising slowly to about two to three thousand feet. During takeoffs and landings, the birds are quite vocal.

Sandhill cranes range across almost all of North America and across a major portion of Canada, through Alaska, and into Siberia. Unfortunately, three of the six races of the sandhill—the greater, lesser, and Canadian—are still legally hunted.

Lillian Annette Rowe Sanctuary

One of the few protected areas for sandhills is the 2,200-acre Lillian Annette Rowe Audubon Sanctuary, along a segment of the Platte River valley in south-central Nebraska. The sanctuary straddles four miles of the Platte that are lined by forests, with cottonwood the dominant tree along the shoreline. The area hosts the largest concentration of lesser sandhill cranes in the world. Approximately 100,000 sandhills roost in the sanctuary from March 10 through April 10 each year; another 400,000 roost around the sanctuary on the Platte River. Dammed and controlled, the Platte is no longer a mile wide; instead, it measures approximately four hundred yards at its very widest and just two hundred yards wide on the average. The sandhills require bare sandbars for roosting, and since the river no longer has the power to wash away woody growth on the bars, the Audubon staff now maintains the sandbars.

The sanctuary is closed to the public except for the one month during spring migration. To see the cranes, visitors must make prior arrangements with Audubon staff. There are two tours a day, one at 5:00 A.M. and the other at 5:00 P.M. Each tour takes three hours. Visitors watch from permanent blinds so as not to disturb the birds, which fly in and out every day.

There is one trail, the Mark Bolin Nature Trail, which is open to the public from Memorial Day to Labor Day. It runs through a native prairie and is not intended for viewing the cranes but, rather, for experiencing the habitat.

To reach the sanctuary, take I-80 to the Gibbon exit #285, drive two miles south on a paved road, then two miles west on a gravel road to the entrance.

Lillian Annette Rowe Sanctuary
Route 2, Box 146
Gibbon, NE 68840
(308) 468-5282

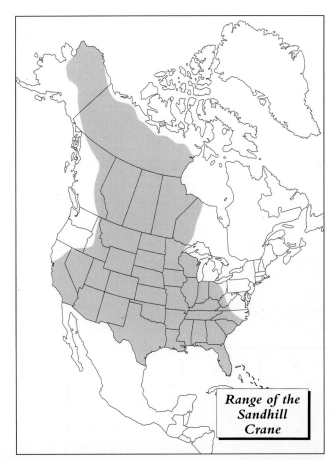

BELOW: *At night cranes roost in shallow water in open areas to avoid predators that might sneak up on land. At sunrise the birds become quite active and fly off for the day's feeding.*

About half a dozen whooping cranes can be found wintering with thousands of sandhill cranes in New Mexico's Bosque del Apache National Wildlife Refuge. OVERLEAF: *Large open fields provide excellent feeding grounds for digging up insects and insect larvae. Open areas like this one allow whooping cranes to see a potential predator long before it can get close enough to pose a threat.*

Whooping Crane
GRUS AMERICANA

Of all the wading birds, the whooping crane stands as a symbol of the lengths to which humankind will go in order to save a species. In the early 1940s, this bird's numbers were down to fewer than thirty; today, because of heroic conservation efforts by the U.S. Fish and Wildlife Service and the National Audubon Society in establishing refuges beneath the cranes' flyways, whooping cranes number over two hundred including captive birds. ● This magnificent bird stands five feet tall with a seven-and-a-half-foot wingspan. Its plumage is white with black primaries and secondaries. It has a bare red crown that extends to mid-crown, much like that of the sandhill; the bird looks like it is wearing a red beret pushed forward onto its forehead. It also has a black mask extending from the base of the large, dull-yellow-green beak to its yellow eyes and cheeks. The whooper's long legs are black, as are its large feet. The whooping crane weighs approximately fifteen pounds — many pounds more than the lesser sandhill crane, which it towers over on the Platte River during migration. ● Whooping cranes apparently require a large nesting and feeding territory, which the male defends aggressively. After selecting a nesting area, the pair will use the same territory year after year. Although a whooping crane bonds for life, it will pair again if its mate dies. ● Prior to mating, the pair perform a unison call that seems to stimulate the female; dancing with wings outstretched may ensue. After copulation, nests are constructed along the edges of small lakes or in shallow water, usually where water is no more than six to sixteen inches in depth. The nests are built of grasses and reeds piled in a large mound with a depression; they may range from two to five feet in diameter. The female lays two buff-colored eggs with brown markings, approximately 98 x 62mm. The male incubates the eggs for most of the day, while the female stays with the eggs at night. Neither bird strays far from the other, keeping watch for possible predators such as coyotes and wolves. ● It takes a little over a month for the two

golden-colored chicks to hatch but within twenty-four hours the young can already swim from the nest. Since whoopers nest in the extreme north, parents may brood the chicks for the first couple of weeks. Adult cranes molt at this time, leaving them flightless; few animals except for wolves, however, can get past the bird's sharp stabbing beak.

The young whoopers learn to hide in thickets at any sign of danger once they attain their white-and-brown mixed plumage. After the bird fledges, it may still be fed by the adults. The young whooper will migrate and feed with its parents until it is approximately one year of age. The juvenile whooping crane will not attain complete adult plumage until its second molt and will not attempt breeding until its fourth or fifth year. The youngster is solid white, stained with brown, and lacks a red crown. In fact, if a red crown were exhibited during the first year, the adult birds would react to this as a stimulus to drive the juvenile from their territory.

Until the mid-1950s, the nesting area of these cranes was not known. Eventually, their remaining nesting area was discovered in northern Canada at Wood Buffalo National Park, some 2,600 miles from their wintering grounds in coastal Texas. Migration from Canada begins in the fall when birds begin to leave in groups of three or more, or sometimes singly. They can fly several hundred miles in a day, usually stopping off in the same areas year after year. One of the better-known stopover sites, where they spend several days feeding and resting, is the Platte River in Nebraska. Their final winter destination is the Aransas National Wildlife Refuge, located on the Blackjack Peninsula on the coast of Texas. The whooping cranes feed along the tidal flats and Intracoastal Waterway, which bisects Aransas, in search of blue crabs, fiddler crabs, shrimp, and other aquatic prey. They also eat acorns from the live oaks, as well as insects and berries.

A second group of whoopers introduced by biologists can be found migrating with sandhills from Grays Lake National Wildlife Refuge in southeastern Idaho to winter at New Mexico's Bosque del Apache National Wildlife Refuge.

More recently, the Patuxant Wildlife Research Center in Maryland, which has a captive breeding program, has released nonmigratory whoopers in the Kissimmee Prairie region in Florida. This gives the species more chances for survival in the event a catastrophe strikes one population. These introduced populations are in locations where whoopers once occurred as native birds, before the wild population was so greatly reduced by shooting and habitat changes over one hundred years ago.

Bosque del Apache National Wildlife Refuge

Just ninety miles south of Albuquerque, New Mexico, is Bosque del Apache National Wildlife Refuge, winter home for thousands of sandhill cranes and snow geese. This wildlife refuge encompasses some 57,191 acres—1,400 of which are planted in corn and winter wheat to attract the birds.

Water impoundments in the refuge have been created by dikes. Some water is pumped in from underground wells, other water diverted from irrigation canals. There is a fifteen-mile, one-way loop road on top of the dikes, which visitors may enter one hour before sunrise and remain on until one hour past sunset. Since the water is pumped in, the ponds are temporary and usually full from around November through February, when most visitors and birds arrive.

Bosque is situated along nine miles of the Rio Grande River at the foot of the Chupadera Mountains. Three of the six races of sandhill crane winter here, all of them migratory, including the Canadian, greater, and lesser. On my visit to the refuge in February 1993, there were six whooping cranes and more than seventeen thousand sandhills. The whoopers travel with their sandhill parents to Bosque, but there never are large numbers as in Aransas. The greater sandhill crane is the more abundant of the three.

To reach Bosque, take I-25 to the San Antonio exit, then turn east on Route 380 until you reach Route 1, where you turn right and travel south approximately eight miles. The refuge headquarters will be on the right, and the refuge entrance on the left.

Bosque del Apache National Wildlife Refuge
P.O. Box 1246
Socorro, NM 87801
(505) 835-1828

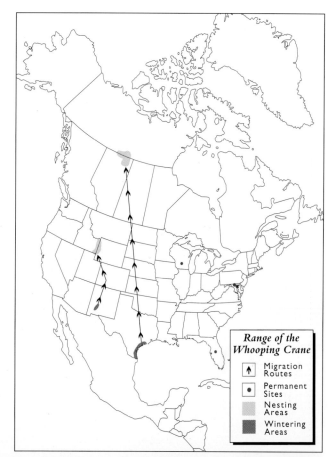

BELOW: *Whooping cranes feed along the tidal flats and Intra-coastal Waterway in search of blue crabs, fiddler crabs (pictured), shrimp, and other aquatic prey.*

Bibliography

Audubon Society Master Guide to Birding, Vol. 1: Loons to Sandpipers, ed. John Farrand, Jr. (1983). New York: Borzoi Books.

Baynard, Oscar E. (1913). "Home Life of the Glossy Ibis." *The Wilson Bulletin,* vol. 25, pp. 103–117.

Bent, Arthur C. (1963). *Life Histories of North American Marsh Birds.* New York: Dover Publications (originally published 1926).

Carr, Archie, and the editors of Time-Life Books. (1973). *The Everglades.* New York: Time-Life Books.

Chapman, Frank M. (1908). *Camps and Cruises of an Ornithologist.* [no publisher cited]

Doughty, Robin W. (1989). *Return of the Whooping Crane.* Austin: University of Texas Press.

Douglas, Marjory Stoneman. (1974). *The Everglades: River of Grass.* New York: Mockingbird Books (originally published 1947).

Eckert, Allan W., and Karl E. Karalus. (1981). *The Wading Birds of North America.* New York: Weathervane Books.

Ehrlich, Paul R., David S. Dobkin, and Darryl Wheye. (1988). *The Birders Handbook: A Field Guide to the Natural History of North American Birds.* New York: Simon and Schuster.

Farrand, John. (1988). *An Audubon Handbook: Eastern Birds.* New York: McGraw-Hill.

Florida Game and Fresh Water Fish Commission. *Florida Atlas of Breeding Sites for Herons and Their Allies.* Technical Report No. 10, Sept. 1991.

Hancock, James, and James Kushlan. (1984). *The Herons Handbook.* London: Croom Helm.

Harrison, Hal H. (1975). *A Field Guide to Birds' Nests.* Boston: Houghton Mifflin.

Johnsgard, Paul A. (1991). *Crane Music.* Washington: Smithsonian Institution Press.

Lane, James A. (1990). *A Birder's Guide to Florida.* Colorado Springs: American Birding Assoc.

Martin, Richard P., and Gary D. Lester. (1990). *Atlas and Census of Wading Birds and Seabird Nesting Colonies in Louisiana: 1990.* Louisiana Dept. of Wildlife and Fisheries. Special Report No. 3.

McNulty, Faith. (1966). *The Whooping Crane: The Bird that Defies Extinction.* New York: E. P. Dutton & Co.

Pettingill, Olin S. (1980). *A Guide to Bird Finding: East of the Mississippi.* Boston: Houghton Mifflin.

Pough, Richard H. (1951). *Audubon Water Bird Guide: Water, Game and Large Land Birds Eastern and Central North America from Southern Texas to Central Greenland.* Illustrated by Don Eckelberry and Earl L. Poole. New York: Doubleday & Company.

Soothill, Eric and Richard. (1982). *Wading Birds of the World.* Poole, Dorset: Blandford Press.

Spendelow, J.D., and S.R. Patton. (1988). *National Atlas of Coastal Waterbird Colonies in the Contiguous United States: 1976–82.* U.S. Fish Wildl. Serv. Biol. Rep. 88(5).

Sprunt, Alexander, John C. Ogden, and Suzanne Winkler. (1978). *Wading Birds.* New York: National Audubon Society.

Terres, John K. (1987). *The Audubon Society Encyclopedia of North American Birds.* New York: Alfred A. Knopf.

A mated pair of wood storks exhibit their courtship ritual, raising their bills into the air and rubbing them together.

INDEX

A green-backed heron stretches out and ruffles its feathers. Just before flying off, the bird may defecate and become quite vocal.

About the Author

Photograph © by Rob Hoffman.

John Netherton, a nature photographer for more than twenty years, lives in Nashville, Tennessee, with his wife Judy; together they have five sons. He has had five books published to date, and is quite excited about his new effort with Voyageur Press, *At the Water's Edge: Wading Birds of North America*. His work has appeared in *Audubon, Natural History, National Wildlife, Nikon World, Modern Photography,* and *Popular Photography*. He is a columnist for *Outdoor Photographer*.

John's photography affirms his personal philosophy of respect for nature and his commitment to recording it with passion and sensitivity.